Designer Knitting
with Kitty Bartholomew

Designer Knitting
with Kitty Bartholomew

By Kitty Bartholomew and Kathy Price-Robinson

Sterling Publishing Co., Inc. New York

A Sterling/Chapelle Book

Chapelle, Ltd.:
Jo Packham, Sara Toliver, Cindy Stoeckl

If you have any questions or comments, please contact:
Chapelle, Ltd., Inc., P.O. Box 9252, Ogden, UT 84409
(801) 621-2777 • (801) 621-2788 Fax
e-mail: chapelle@chapelleltd.com
Web site: www.chapelleltd.com

A Red Lips 4 Courage Book
Red Lips 4 Courage Communications, Inc.
8502 E. Chapman Ave., 303
Orange, CA 92869
Web site: www.redlips4courage.com

Library of Congress Cataloging-in-Publication Data

Bartholomew, Kitty.
  Designer knitting with Kitty Bartholomew / Kitty Bartholomew and Kathy Price-Robinson.
      p. cm.
  "A Sterling/Chapelle book"
  Includes index.
  ISBN 1-4027-2611-2
  1. Knitting--Patterns. 2. Sweaters. I. Price-Robinson, Kathy. II. Title.

TT825.B35 2005
746.43'20432--dc22
                                                                                    2005013024

10 9 8 7 6 5 4 3 2 1
Published by Sterling Publishing Co., Inc.
387 Park Ave. South, New York, NY 10016
©2005 Kitty Bartholomew and Kathy Price-Robinson
Distributed in Canada by Sterling Publishing
c/o Canadian Manda Group, 165 Dufferin St.
Toronto, Ontario, Canada M6K 3H6
Distributed in Great Britain by Chrysalis Books Group PLC, The Chrysalis Building,
Bramley Road, London W10 6SP, England
Distributed in Australia by Capricorn Link (Australia) Pty. Ltd.
P.O. Box 704, Windsor, NSW 2756, Australia
Printed and Bound in China
All Rights Reserved
Sterling ISBN 1-4027-2611-2

For information about custom editions, special sales, premium and corporate purchases, please contact Sterling Special Sales Department at (800)805-5489 or specialsales@sterlingpub.com.

Foreword

MY FRIEND, THE KNITTER

Kitty and I have worked together, traveled together, and hung out together since we first met backstage at ABC's "Home Show" in 1988.

That's me on the left with my longtime friend and passionate knitter, Kitty.

She is a fun friend to have because she is so full of surprises. Who else would think of tying belts around chair seat edges to make a seat? Or weave ties in and out to accomplish the same thing? Or cut up men's suits (purchased at thrift stores) to hook a rug?

Her imagination and creativity seem boundless. I was even surprised to discover at least six years into our friendship that Kitty had a secret passion for knitting. Knitting? I'd never even seen her with a pair of needles in her hands but now she was turning out sweaters at the rate of about one a week—without a pattern, and with more than just one yarn at a time.

Kitty came to a party wearing a simple black sweater polka dotted with pearls that had everybody oohing and aahing. Nobody believed she made it; I knew that she had.

The same free spirit Kitty shows when she puts belts on chairs and turns men's suits into rugs is evident in her knitting. Kitty can see mohair, ribbon, and a novelty yarn not individually, but together. She can alter a pattern by making the turtleneck longer, or shorter. She can give a sweater a whole new look by changing the ribbing. She recently made a scarf from a flannel nightgown!

And now, she has put down her needles long enough to write a book about some of her creations, to inspire you to free up your own creativity and imagination. If there is a sweater on the following pages that you like but would prefer with a longer hem, or a different yarn, Kitty will cheer you on and give you the freedom to make those changes.

Knitting may be the hot trend these days but Kitty is not following the trend...She's simply doing what she loves to do.

—Carol Duvall

Table of Contents

Introduction

SAVORING THE PROCESS

Knitting is a high for me. Some people eat chocolate. Some go shopping. I knit. With this high, I get something else: beautiful, chic, handmade sweaters that are too easy and simple to believe. I've learned how to knit sweaters that fit, sweaters that flatter, and sweaters that are fun to design and make.

For me, knitting is not just an emotional high. The process of knitting affects my entire being. I can think more clearly when I knit; my thoughts are collected. And the sensuousness of the yarns! Sometimes my fingers start to itch when I see certain yarns. I want to touch them. I don't just focus on the sweater I will end up with; I savor the process. When I'm working with yarns I love, each stitch is like a kiss.

My grandmother taught me to knit when I was a little girl. I worked on doll blankets then, with my back to a lighthouse on Grosse Isle, Michigan, where all I could see in front of me was open water. Knitting helped me sort out a growing girl's thoughts. In high school, I bought my first sweater kit and felt proud as my grandmother helped me through the complicated pattern and

complex stitches. I even knitted a sweater for a boyfriend, though he couldn't get it over his head.

I put down my knitting for many years. I went to college, worked in the fashion industry, traveled around Europe, and started my family. By the late 1980s, I began appearing on TV as an interior decorator. It was during the taping of my early shows—waiting for crews to fiddle with the lighting or get the set ready—that I developed an overwhelming desire to knit. I woke up one morning and there it was—an unexpected, unanticipated, nearly insatiable craving to get my hands on yarn.

So much had changed between then and the day my grandmother placed the first set of needles in my little hands. I had changed and the world of knitting had changed. In

my grandmother's day, needles were thin and so were the yarns. The only way to knit was to make little stitches, and the fashion of the time was to make complicated patterns using these teeny, intricate stitches. Did you know there's a book that shows 1,000 different stitches?

Well, this kind of knitting was not for me. I had become a respected interior decorator, and I had confidence in my choices of materials and colors for homes. So why not with knitting? I always liked my hands-on projects—stylish yet quick and fun, rather than tedious. So I jumped happily into the yarns available, excited about the new colors, textures, and qualities. I picked up bigger needles, sizes 10 and 11, and I started knitting again with a passion.

I have the courage to create. I don't know where I got this courage, but I know I've strengthened it by using it. If I have a pattern that calls for a ribbing of Knit 1, Purl 1, I have no fear of trying a Knit 1, Purl 2 ribbing. I don't even mind trying a Knit 2,

Purl 6 ribbing. If I don't like it, I can unravel it. If the pattern calls for a ribbing 2" long, I might make it 4" long if I prefer. After all, if the pattern calls for a sweater that's a total of 18" long, who's to say that 4" or 2" of that should be ribbing? I decide. I design.

When I returned to knitting, I also started mixing yarns. What great fun this is. To take various colors and types, widths and styles, and blend them into never-seen-before combinations is beyond wonderful. I often look at two yarns at the yarn shop, wonder how they would look together, and stand there and knit a small piece. If I like what I see, I buy the yarn. There's no need to wait until someone tells us which yarns look chic together. We decide. We design.

I want my sweaters to look handmade, not homemade. I want a sweater that looks as if it came from Barneys New York or Neiman Marcus. One difference between a sweater I could buy off the rack at the finest store and the one I knit by hand is that my sweater fits me perfectly. I like sweaters to fit; I abhor sloppy. At a good knit shop, they can measure your arms, your chest, and your trunk, and then whip up a pattern for a sweater that's perfect for you.

The purpose of this book is to convey the joy I get from knitting gorgeous, well-fitting sweaters to inspire you to embrace this same thrilling and productive activity. As you will see, the patterns in this book are pretty basic. I have also knitted a few sweaters that are more complex, and I'm proud of those sweaters. But I left them out because I want to share the easy, fast, and fun sweaters that are my favorites.

My hope is that as you read this book, you will enjoy seeing my sweaters and reading about what inspired them and how I added my own twists. Rather than copy one of my projects, think about mixing your own yarns and altering a basic pattern to suit you, and then knit up your own masterpiece.

Tailor basic patterns that reflect your taste and mix yarns in unique ways to make sweaters that fit you. I want you to see how great a hand-knit sweater can look. The goal in sharing my enthusiasm and successes in handknitting is to get you inspired to make the choices that make sense for you.

One of my pet peeves in other knitting books is when photos of yarn don't match those used in the projects. Each project in my book shows a photo of the yarns I used. You may wish to use other yarns. You may find inspiration in some of the other yarn photos scattered throughout other parts of the book.

So, let's get started.

Citty Bartholomew

(Opposite) I spend a lot of money on yarn and a lot of time crafting my sweaters, so the results of my labor and investment should fit me.

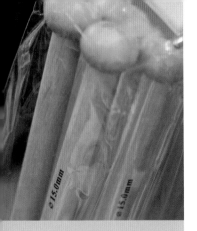

(Above) The days of knitting with tiny needles have given way to larger needles that make knitting much more enjoyable.

(Opposite) Sometimes I choose my next yarn just by walking through the store and seeing what catches my eye.

YARNS: A LOVE STORY

After making a few sweaters in high school, I'd pretty much given up on knitting until that day, more than 10 years ago, when I woke up with an itching to feel yarn between my fingers.

At the yarn store, I was awed by the vast array of colors and textures—thick and thin, shiny and multicolored, fat and delicate, wools and cottons, blends, ribbons, and cords. This was a far cry from the solid-colored wool yarns of my childhood, yarns that called for size 6 needles, or smaller.

These new yarns, worked on size 10, 11,

13, or 15 needles, opened up the world of knitting for me. When I discovered I didn't have to put my sweaters together myself, that I could pay the yarn shop to do it for me (see To Finish or Not to Finish? page 20), I was off and running.

I'd like to show you some of the yarns I've used for the sweaters in this book. Later I will show you how I've combined yarns to create unique looks and textures for my sweaters. Here I've separated the yarns into categories so you can consider the qualities of each.

CONSIDER THIS
Getting the Right Size

In the basic instructions for each project, the small size indicates the size of the original sweater. Figures for larger sizes are also included to help you design your own version of the sweater. If you knit one of the larger sizes or make the garment longer, be sure to purchase enough extra yarn to complete your project. Your yarn shop can help you determine how much extra yarn you may need. It's better to buy too much, especially if the shop allows you to return unstarted skeins. Running short can trigger creative thinking, but it won't allow you to make the sweater you set out to knit. For larger sizes, because of the larger armhole, the underarm sweater length will be a bit shorter than for the small size shown. The total length from lower edge to shoulder remains the same, unless you make other adjustments.

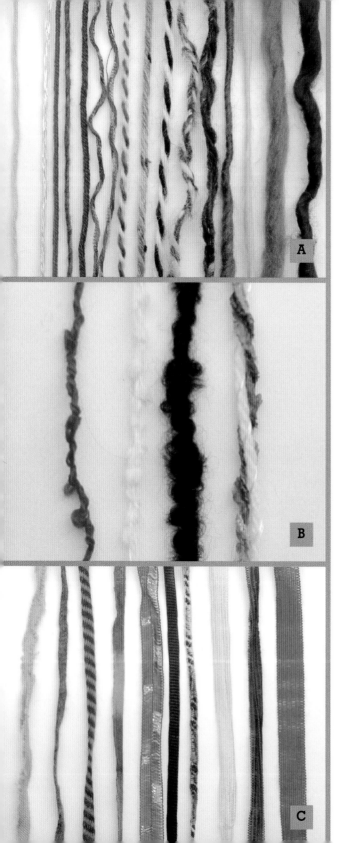

Basic wool and cotton blends (A)

Generally speaking, I like my sweaters to have some substance, some meat, some "hand," as a number of knitters refer to it. Back in the day when mohair sweaters were all the rage, soft and delicate sweaters were common. But for my money, I want more bulk. I usually get this with a wool or cotton blend as my starting point.

When I first came back to knitting, the fat yarns got my attention. I used great big size 13 needles and my sweaters were fun and fast. Later on, I got more creative and wanted to mix various yarns, so I started with a thinner basic wool or cotton blend and combined other yarns to create unique looks. I generally try to combine yarns to make a gauge of 2 to 3 stitches per inch using size 11 needles. That feels right to me.

I like wool best because it retains its shape and wears well. Many yarns are a combination of wool and/or cotton and/or synthetic and/or other fibers, and this gives you many fine qualities all in the same strand. Wools are very serviceable, very durable. They take you from a morning trimming rose bushes to a night out at the movies.

You could almost trace my progress in my new sweater passion from right to left in this photo, with the fat purple and green wools used for my Random Purl Turtlenecks in Chapter Three on the right. The thin blue yarn at the left was used for my Blue Cable V-Neck in Chapter Four, one of my latest creations.

Boucles (B)

Boucle (pronounced boo-CLAY) is a type of yarn with three strands, one of which is looser and wraps around the other two. I find myself using boucles because of the interesting texture, and because it gives my pieces substance. The big and fat black boucle you see here helped give my Black Multi-Tweed cardigan in Chapter Two its bear-like quality, while the white cotton boucle helped add substance to my Red-Sleeve Scotland cardigan in the same chapter. The red boucle was a nice balance to the mohair in my Red Tweed with Contrasting Neck turtleneck sweater in Chapter Three.

Ribbons (C)

I am fairly new to the world of ribbons, and it's a wonderful world to live in. I would hardly even call it a yarn, but that's how it's referred to. It is not twisted; it's flat, lighter weight, and has a sheen to it, so it has a completely different hand, a different touch. Ribbon yarns tend to be a bit dressier.

Wools are more workhorse, more utilitarian, more practical. A sweater made of all ribbon or some ribbon will be a bit more fragile, and there is a possibility of snagging. You definitely wouldn't want to haul firewood in a ribbon sweater.

As for the texture, feeling, and visual interest of ribbons, I am intrigued by them and I've done a fair amount of experimenting with them. I used the red ribbon shown here for my Long Red Ribbon cardigan in Chapter Two, and the multicolored ribbon in my Brown and Khaki Cable V-Neck sweater in Chapter Four.

See that gorgeous hot pink ribbon with the metallic flecks? Believe it or not, that is a wool blend, so it's going to be very durable. I used it with a thin hot pink mohair to make my daughter the Evening Shawl in Chapter Five.

Novelty (D)

So what is novelty yarn? As far as I can figure, it's any yarn that doesn't fit neatly into other categories. I love novelty yarns and make good use of them. However, they can be expensive, so you'll want to mix them with other, less expensive yarns to add substance and durability.

The flag yarns pictured here (the ones with the long flags hanging off a base of mohair) are a good example of this. Knitting a sweater of just this thin yarn, on tiny needles, would drive me nuts. So I mixed it with a strong basic wool yarn for an interesting look.

Check out the chenille in this photo, which I used for my Gray Chenille cardigan in Chapter Two with the silk ribbons. The aqua novelty yarn on the right is what gives my Aqua Silver turtleneck in Chapter Three its pizzazz.

Softies (E)

I call these softies, but they are technically the mohairs, cashmeres, and angoras that give so many of my sweaters their coziness without adding too much bulk. There was a time when women and girls would knit sweaters out of all mohair, with thin needles. I used mohair to add fluffiness to my Aqua Silver turtleneck, to cut down the brightness of the multicolored cotton in my Pumpkin Patch pullover in Chapter One, to blend with a rust wool in my Basic Rust Mohair pullover in the same chapter, and to add coziness to my Scotland cardigans in Chapter Two. I created my Scotland sweaters when I was in Scotland, and of course you want to add mohair in a situation like that.

I did make a whole sweater with a softie, my cashmere Sherbet Scoop Neck pullover in Chapter One. I made it more interesting by creating a series of stripes that start big on the bottom of the sweater and get narrower on top. I like this sweater, but I prefer to add mohairs and cashmeres to more substantial yarns.

Off-Beat (F)

These are yarns that wouldn't come to mind when you think about knitting. But why not? You can knit with anything. Here, I'm showing you the off-beat yarns I've used in this book. I knit a vest out of torn cotton fabric. I knit a book bag for my teenage daughter out of common jute twine you can find at the hardware store.

I've also made a couple of scarves and a placemat from strips of old flannel nightgowns. In fact, if you have a favorite piece of clothing that has a rip, stain, or is tattered, try tearing it into strips, tying the strips end to end, and knitting something out of it. After all, as I've been known to say, "It's not what you don't have, it's what you do with what you do have."

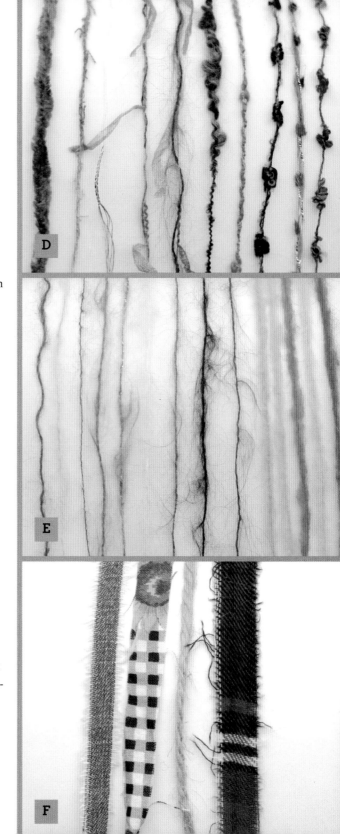

(Above) I started out with a thin green wool on this piece and ended with a multicolored novelty yarn.

COMBINING YARNS

To show you how much fun it is to combine yarns, I sat down and knit four swatches, adding and subtracting various yarns as I went along. This was fun, fun, fun. In fact, you might find this an enjoyable exercise to do with some of the extra yarns you have lying around. You never know what a mohair is going to do to the look of a novelty ribbon, for instance, unless you knit them together and experience the result yourself.

You might notice that I'm not telling you the exact brand, name, and color of the yarns I've used in these swatches. The idea is for you to free up your creative self, to combine yarns in ways that nobody has tried before. The basic idea is to combine yarns so they highlight each other, rather than cancel each other out. For instance, two multicolored novelty yarns in yellow tones will probably cancel each other out, and that might be a waste of money if they are expensive. But mixing one multicolored novelty yarn in yellow tones with a green mohair might just make each yarn more interesting than if each stood alone.

I generally start with a basic wool or cotton to add substance to the finished piece, and then add various ribbon, boucles, mohairs, or novelty yarns as the spirit moves me.

To find out for yourself what moves you, experimenting is key. It is much easier (and more cost effective) to test on a swatch than a whole sweater. Here's what I've come up with. How about you?

Combination 1: Green

1. To begin, I cast 20 stitches onto a size 8 needle using a thin green wool. This would make a lightweight sweater that's ideal for summer.

2. I changed to size 10 needles and added a very thin beige ribbon, similar to the ribbon in my Brown and Khaki Cable V-Neck in Chapter Four. Look at the interest this adds. I consider this a good summer weight.

3. Keeping my size 10 needles, I eliminated the ribbon and added a green boucle to my thin green wool. The texture this creates is quite unique.

4. Here I added back in the beige ribbon with the wool and boucle. The three yarns together create a thicker overall strand, so I moved up to size 11 needles to keep the stitches from getting too tight.

5. To create some softness, I added a green mohair to the wool and boucle. This is the same green mohair I used to tone down the multicolored boucle for my Pumpkin Patch pullover in Chapter One. A sweater made of mohair, wool, and boucle would still be light, but cozy enough for fall or winter.

6. Finally, I added multicolored novelty yarn. This is my idea of heaven. This is a Kitty sweater. It looks good and it feels good.

Combination 2: Purple

1. To begin, I cast 20 stitches onto a size 8 needle using a thin purple ribbon. This creates a somewhat silky fabric that would be great for a light-weight sweater.

2. Switching to size 10 needles, I added in a novelty yarn that looks like two delicate strings joined with tiny silky panels. Now the fabric has a sheen and texture that is nighttime dressy, which is great for a shell.

3. For warmth, I added in a multicolored mohair and switched to size 11 needles. This cuts the sheen a little and adds some elegance.

4. To the ribbon, novelty string, and mohair I added a fourth yarn, a curly mohair loop. It has all the elements I like: color, texture, and interest. It's a real "go for it" combination. All of these yarns together called for a switch to size 15 needles.

5. Keeping with size 15 needles, I changed the purple mohair loop to a rust mohair loop. I love the way the satin squares on the ribbon yarn occasionally pop up in the mohair.

Combination 3: Blue and Red

1. To begin, I cast 20 stitches onto a size 8 needle using a thin blue ribbon. This is the same blue I used as an accent in my Colorful Tennis cardigan in Chapter Two.

2. Switching to size 10 ½ needles, I added a mohair in the same blue color. This is a soft, basic yarn that is very complimentary.

3. I then added a multicolored boucle, using size 13 needles, to the blue ribbon and blue mohair to see what would happen. Now we've got the substance of the ribbon, the tactile pleasure of the mohair, and the interest of the boucle.

4. Keeping my size 13 needles and the multicolored boucle, I switched to a red ribbon (which I used for my Long Red Ribbon cardigan in Chapter Two) and basic thin, red wool. Notice that the same multicolored yarn can blend with many colors. The red changed the look of the boucle.

5. Without the boucle, I mixed the red wool and ribbon with a red mohair and went down to size 11 needles. This might make a basic red sweater, but it's so much more interesting than using just one yarn.

6. Finally, I wanted to show the combination of a red ribbon and a basic wool on size 10 needles, without the mohair.

(Above) On this piece, I started with a thin purple ribbon and ended with a rust mohair loop.

(Below) A thin blue ribbon was used at the top of this piece, which ends with a combination of a red ribbon and a basic wool.

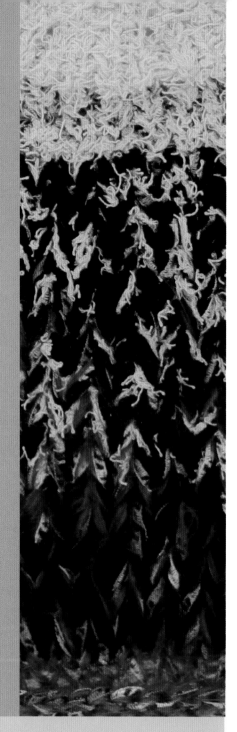

(Above) I started this piece using a cotton cream-colored novelty rag and finished it off with a multicolored ribbon and mohair.

Combination 4: Beige and Rust

1. To begin, I cast 20 stitches onto a size 8 needle using a cotton novelty rag. This is a cream-colored version of the blue rag I used in my Denim Turtle with Twisted Braid turtleneck in Chapter Three.

2. Switching to size 10 needles, I added in a multicolored tape, which I also used in my Brown and Khaki Cable V-Neck in Chapter Four. Notice how the yellow in the tape disappears against the cream rag.

3. With size 13 needles, I added in a rather thick black boucle, which is the same yarn I used in the Black Multi-Tweed cardigan you'll find in Chapter Two. I think these three yarns would be great in a blanket.

4. To the rag, tape, and boucle, I added a rust mohair, switching to size 15 needles to accommodate the growing thickness of the overall strand. This is the same rust mohair I used in my Basic Rust Mohair pullover in Chapter One. Notice how the rust mohair picks up the rust tones in the multi-colored ribbon.

5. Next, staying with size 15 needles, I took out the cream rag to see how the mohair, boucle, and ribbon would look together. Without the rag, the ribbon stands out more. If you're going to pay a lot for yarn, you don't want it to disappear in your fabric.

6. Finally, switching back to size 10 needles, I paired the multicolored ribbon with the mohair. This would make a yummy evening shawl or light summer sweater.

TO FINISH OR NOT TO FINISH?

If you're like me, you absolutely revel in the process of choosing or creating your sweater design, experimenting with luscious yarns to find the most wonderful combinations, and indulging in the sheer joy of knitting your sweater, the fibers moving through your fingers, the continuous surprise of the piece growing in your hands.

However, like me, you might not find such joy in finishing the sweater. By that I mean sewing the sides together, sewing on the sleeves, making the collar, if there is one, making the buttonholes, and so on. I can finish sweaters, but it's not how I want to spend my time. Instead, I take my sweater to the yarn shop and pay them to finish it.

Typically a yarn shop works with talented finishers that may take the sweaters home to work on. I've found that it takes one or two weeks to get a sweater finished, and the cost is based on the complexity of what you want done. Some knitters want a fringe put on a poncho, others want an edge crocheted onto a baby blanket. If you are going to pay for this service, you'll want to knit a sweater out of high-quality yarn so you will get years of enjoyment out of your piece.

Even if you don't live near a yarn shop, you can mail your knitted pieces (usually the front, back, and sleeves) to a quality yarn shop to be finished. Depending on the shop, you might want to call ahead and discuss your needs and get a quote. Often, the pattern you are using will have all the finishing details needed, so you don't have to be a knitting genius to have your hand-knit pieces professionally assembled.

To finish or not to finish? Personally, I'd rather turn in one knitted sweater, leave it to someone else to finish, and then move on to the next glorious project.

YARNS USED IN THESE PROJECTS

Because some of these sweaters were made over a period of time, and the original yarns were purchased at several places here and overseas, we have given only general descriptions of the yarns actually used with the individual project instructions. This will help you begin your own creation by combining the yarns you find available at your own yarn shop. Additional suggestions are listed at the back of the book with specific yarns suggested.

Once you have selected your yarns, you will need to check your gauge to the gauge in the instructions. If they don't match, try different needle sizes or adjust the weight of the yarns. The latter is easier to do if you keep the novelty yarns selected and change the weight of the basic yarn, if possible, selecting a lighter weight sport yarn in the same color to replace a knitting-worsted weight yarn, for instance. You can also see if the instructions for the next larger or smaller garment size will give the finished size you want.

To check the instructions for the new size, divide the number of stitches for the back (just below the armhole shaping) by the number of stitches you get per inch with your selected yarns. If the resulting size (width of back) is right for you, use the directions for that size.

If you are an experienced knitter, select the yarns you like, work on the needle size that gives you the best "hand" for the selected yarns, and cast on the number of stitches you need to make the width of the piece you need to fit, following the instructions only as a general guide for shaping and style.

Most of the sweaters are simply shaped, so you will find it easier than you thought to adjust the design for your own unique sweater.

(Above) Sometimes it's just easier having your local knit shop finish your piece for you.

(Below) With so many yarns available, the sweaters you can design are endless.

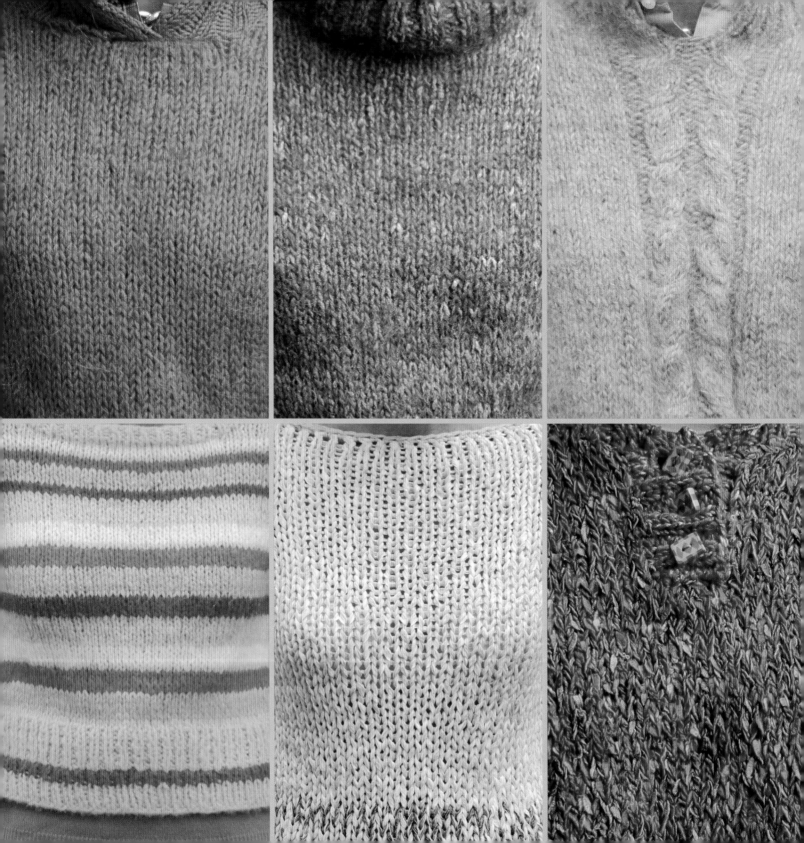

Pullovers

In this chapter, I will show you some of my very favorite sweaters. At a quick glance, you might think these are all very different patterns. But there are really just two basic patterns: the boatneck and the mock turtleneck. All of the variations you see are from using somewhat courageous combinations of yarns and variations in neck length, sleeve length, and ribbing. Rather than copy my choices exactly, think about how you can remake these into your own fashion statement. For instance, in this chapter you'll see my idea of good fun: a striped boatneck made from luscious cashmere yarn. What color stripes would you enjoy? What sleeve length would feel best to you? What pants need a complementary sweater? When you vary the colors and yarns, necks and ribs, you are in that exalted category of "sweater designer." Enjoy the status.

Pullover Projects:

1. Basic Rust Mohair
2. Pumpkin Patch
3. Taupe Angora Tweed
4. Sherbet Scoop Neck
5. Reversible Boatneck
6. Carnival

Project 1

BASIC RUST MOHAIR PULLOVER

I start with this sweater because it has turned out to be the one I wear most. When I knitted it, I thought it would be just another sweater, but it ended up going with everything. It is not a true red; it is more like a terra-cotta rust so it coordinates with reds, blacks, and browns. What really turned out better than I ever imagined was combining two yarns, one a typical wool and one a mohair. The twist is that I didn't use the mohair on the collar, sleeve ribbing, or bottom edge. When I smooth it around my waist, the ribbing has a wonderful bounce to it.

(Above) I used merino wool mixed with mohair in the exact same shade of rust.

(Opposite) The open collar allows me to wear the Basic Rust Mohair over a shirt or turtleneck, or by itself.

Garment Sizes

36" (38", 40") to fit 34" (36", 38") body measurement at bust
Width of back at underarm: 18" (19", 20")
Length to shoulder: 18"
Sleeve length: 18"

Materials

Needles: 1 pair size 9 (5.5 mm) needles, 1 pair size 13 (9 mm) needles or size needed to obtain gauge, 16"-long circular needle size 9 (5.5 mm) for collar
Yarn: The original yarns used for this project were a fine quality knitting-worsted weight wool yarn (yarn A) and a mohair yarn (yarn B). Yarn A was used alone for the ribbed edges and both yarns A and B were used together for the body of the sweater.

Gauge

2.9 stitches per inch, 4 rows per inch, on larger needles

Basic Instructions

Back: On smaller needles, cast on 68 (72, 76) stitches with yarn A. Work in Knit 2, Purl 2 rib for 3". Change to larger needles and attach yarn B. Working with both A and B yarns, knit across, decreasing 16 (17, 18) stitches evenly spaced across first row 52 (55, 58) stitches. Starting with Purl row on wrong side, work in Stockinette stitch until piece measures 18" in length. Bind off 17 (18, 19) stitches loosely at beginning of next 2 rows. Slip remaining 18 (19, 20) stitches on stitch holder to work later with collar.

Front: Work same as back until piece measures 16 ½" (or 2 ½" less than back), ending with wrong-side row.

Shape Neck: Work first 21 (22, 23) stitches, drop old yarns, attach another ball of yarns A and B and with new yarns, Knit center 10 (11, 12) stitches, and slip these stitches on stitch holder; Knit to end of row. Working each side of neck with its own

CONSIDER THIS

Choosing Sleeve Length

One of my pet peeves in life is sweaters that have sleeves that are too long for my arms, sleeves that are always getting in the way. I don't want to have to pull my sleeve up to see my watch. I don't want to have to roll up my sleeves. Making my own sweaters allows me to have the perfect sleeve length. How about you? Do you like longer sleeves? Shorter sleeves? What's your pleasure? You decide. You design.

separate yarns, bind off 2 stitches at each neck edge once, then decrease 1 stitch at each neck edge every other row twice. Work even on 17 (18, 19) stitches on each side until piece measures same length as back. Bind off remaining stitches on each side loosely.

Sleeves: On smaller needles, loosely cast on 28 (28, 32) stitches with yarn A. Work in Knit 2, Purl 2 ribbing for 3". Change to larger needles and attach yarn B. Working with both yarns A and B, work in Stockinette stitch, increasing 1 stitch at each edge on next row, then every eighth row 5 (6, 5) times more. Work even on 40 (42, 44) stitches until sleeve measures 18" or length desired to underarm. Bind off all stitches loosely.

Finishing: Sew shoulder seams. Mark side edges of front and back 6 ¼" (6 ½", 6 ¾") from shoulder seam. Matching center of sleeve to shoulder seam, sew top edge of sleeve to sweater between side arm-

hole markers. Sew sleeve and underarm seams.

Collar: With right side of sweater facing you, using circular needle, start at front neck edge to transfer 6 (6, 7) stitches from front stitch holder to needle (use those stitches closest to right front of garment, leaving remaining stitches on holder). Attach yarn A and Knit these 6 (6, 7) stitches, then pick up 12 (13, 14) stitches along right front neck edge to shoulder; Knit 18 (19, 20) stitches from back holder, pick up 12 (13, 14) stitches along left front edge, Knit remaining 4 (5, 5) stitches from front holder, then for overlap at center front, reach behind first stitches of collar to pick up another stitch in each of the first 2 original stitches worked. Work back and forth on 54 (58, 62) stitches in rib as follows: *Row 1:* (right side of folded-down collar): Work in Knit 2, Purl 2 rib, ending with Knit 2. *Row 2:* Purl 2, then work in Knit 2, Purl 2 rib to end. Repeat these 2 rows for 4". Bind off all stitches loosely in ribbing.

(Left) I've added mohair just to the body, leaving the neck and ribbing smooth.

(Clockwise from left) Without the mohair that is in the body, the waist ribbing has more resiliency; the collar does not include the mohair that is in the body of the sweater; the cuff ribbing also does not include mohair.

Project 2

PUMPKIN PATCH PULLOVER

My inspiration for this sweater came from a great pair of pants that really needed something special to go with them. Sure, you can wear black with almost anything. But I wanted something more colorful for fall. So I took these pants into my knit shop and I walked around, looking for inspiration. And I got it. I loved a wonderful cotton orange, blue, gray, and tan tweed yarn. Yet it was a bit too bright for my needs. So when I saw a wonderful gray-green mohair I decided the two mixed together would give me the perfect color.

(Above) The brightness of the novelty boucle with gold threads is tempered by the olive green mohair.

(Opposite) I've always considered this my rainy-day sweater. It's so warm and perfect for the fall.

Garment Sizes

36" (38", 40", 42") to fit 34" (36", 38", 40") body measurement at bust
Width of back at underarm: 18" (19", 20", 21")
Length to shoulder: 18"
Sleeve length: 16"

Materials

Needles: 1 pair size 17 (12.75 mm) needles or size needed to obtain gauge, 16"-long circular needle size 11 (8 mm) for neckband
Yarn: The original yarns used in this project were a sportweight nubby yarn in variegated colors orange, blue, gray, and tan (yarn A) and a mohair yarn in khaki green (yarn B). Both yarns A and B were used together throughout the sweater.

Gauge

3 stitches per inch, 4.5 rows per inch, on larger needles

Basic Instructions

Back: On larger needles, cast on 52 (56, 60, 60) stitches with yarns A and B held together. Work in Knit 2, Purl 2 rib for 2", increasing 2 (1, 0, 3) stitches on last row. Continuing with both yarns, work in Stockinette stitch on 54 (57, 60, 63) stitches until piece measures 11" (10 ¾", 10 ½", 10 ¾") in length.

Shape Armholes: Bind off 3 stitches at beginning of next 2 rows. Decrease 1 stitch at each side every other row 4 times. Work even on 40 (43, 46, 49) stitches until piece measures 18" in length. Bind off all stitches loosely.

Front: Work same as back until piece measures 16" (or 2" less than back), ending with wrong-side row.

Shape Neck: Work first 14 (15, 16, 17) stitches, drop old yarns, attach new yarns A and B and with new yarns, bind off center 12 (13, 14, 15) stitches;

work to end of row. Working each side of neck with its own separate yarns, bind off 3 stitches at each neck edge once, then decrease 1 stitch at each neck edge every other row 3 times. Work even on 8 (9, 10, 11) stitches until piece measures same length as back. Bind off remaining stitches on each side loosely.

Sleeves: On larger needles, cast on 24 (24, 28, 28) stitches with yarns A and B. Work in Knit 2, Purl 2 rib for 2 ½". Change to larger needles and continuing with both yarns A and B, work in Stockinette stitch, increasing 1 stitch at each edge on next row, then every eighth row 4 (5, 4, 5) times more. Work even on 34 (36, 38, 40) stitches until sleeve measures 16".

Shape Cap: Bind off 3 stitches at beginning of next

2 rows. Decrease 1 stitch at each side every other row until cap measures 4". Bind off 3 stitches at beginning of next 4 rows. Bind off all remaining stitches loosely.

Finishing: Sew shoulder seams.

Neckband: With right side of work facing you, using circular needle and both yarns A and B, start at left front shoulder to pick up 76 (76, 80, 80) stitches evenly spaced around neck edge. Join stitches and work in rounds in Knit 2, Purl 2 rib for 2". Bind off all stitches loosely in ribbing. Sew underarm seams; sew sleeve seams. For each sleeve, match center of sleeve to shoulder seam and sew cap of sleeve to shaped armholes of sweater.

(Left) Mixing two different yarns to get the right color lets me create the perfect match to a unique pant color or shoe.

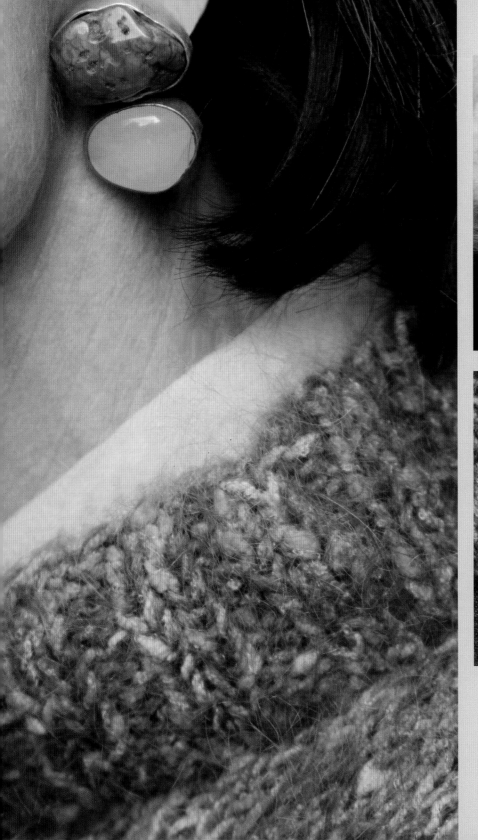

(Clockwise from left) I'm a nut for softness—you can see my soft flannel shirt peeking above the mock turtleneck; the cuff is simple, so as not to distract from the colors and texture of the sweater; this sweater perfectly matches a unique hue of a favorite pair of pants.

31

Project 3

TAUPE ANGORA TWEED PULLOVER

Knock on my door at home and you'll find me in jeans. For this sweater, I wanted something I could throw over a turtleneck, blouse, or knit shirt, something I could wear to a soccer game or around town. Notice that the neck is open, which allows my shirts to peak out. I love the flexibility of this blue and gray heather yarn that coordinates with browns and grays, and it especially goes with jeans. Here's the happy outcome: this sweater also works well with dressier gray pants.

(Above) The blue-gray heather tweed wool gives strength and color, and the taupe angora gives softness.

(Opposite) This sweater is both elegant and cozy, perfect for an al fresco dinner.

Garment Sizes
38" (41", 44") to fit loosely 34" (37", 40") body measurement at bust
Length to shoulder: 18"
Sleeve length: 17"

Materials
Needles: 1 pair size 9 (5.5 mm) needles, 1 pair size 10 ½ (6.5 mm) needles or size needed to obtain gauge, cable needle, 16"-long circular needle size 9 (5.5 mm) for neckband
Yarn: The original yarn used in this project was a chunky weight yarn, a blend of angora with a blue-gray heather tweed. (You can blend your own with a lightweight heather tweed and an angora, or mohair for soft texture.) This yarn was used throughout the sweater.

Gauge
3 stitches per 1", 4.8 rows per inch, in Stockinette stitch on larger needles

Cable Panel
Worked on 14 stitches.
Row 1 (right side): Purl 2, Knit 4, Purl 2, Knit 4, Purl 2
Row 2 and all wrong-side rows: Knit 2, Purl 4, Knit 2, Purl 4, Knit 2
Row 3: Repeat Row 1
Row 5: Repeat Row 1
Row 7 (cable twist): Purl 2, Slip 2 stitches to cable needle and hold in front of work, Knit 2, Knit 2 from cable needle (cable twists to left), Purl 2, Slip 2 stitches to cable needle and hold in back of work, Knit 2, Knit 2 from cable needle (cable twists to right), Purl 2
Row 8: Repeat Row 2
Repeat these 8 rows for cable panel.

Basic Instructions
Back: On smaller straight needles, cast on 62 (68, 74) stitches. Work in Knit 1, Purl 1 rib for 3". Change to larger needles and work in Stockinette

I chose a modest ribbing at the waist.

stitch until piece measures 10" (9 ½", 9") in length, ending in a Purl row.

Shape Armholes: Work decreases as follows: *Row 1 (right side):* (Note: For Cable 2 Back, Slip 1 stitch to cable needle and hold in back of work, Knit 1, Knit 1 from cable needle; for Cable 2 Front, Slip 1 stitch to cable needles and hold in front of work, Knit 1, Knit 1 from cable needle.) To work row, Purl 1, Knit 1, Purl 1, Cable 2 Back, Cable 2 Front, Slip Slip Knit (decrease made,) work to last 9 stitches, Knit 2 Together (another decrease), Cable 2 Front, Cable 2 Back, Purl 1, Knit 1, Purl 1. *Row 2:* Knit 1, Purl 1, Knit 1, Purl to last 3 stitches, Knit 1, Purl 1, Knit 1. Repeat these 2 rows, always decreasing on right-side row 5 times more. Then, without decreasing, continue the 7-stitch cable pattern as established at each armhole, work even on 50 (56, 62) stitches until armholes measure 8" (8 ½", 9"). Bind off 13 (15, 17) stitches beginning of next 2 rows. Slip remaining 24 (26, 28) stitches onto stitch holder.

Front: Work ribbing same as back. Change to larger needles. *Next row (right side):* Knit and increase in first stitch, Knit next 24 (27, 30) stitches, place marker on needle, * Purl 2, Knit 1, Knit and increase in next stitch, Knit 1; repeat from * once more, Purl 2, place another marker on needle, Knit to last stitch, Knit and increase in last stitch 66 (72, 78) stitches. Starting with Row 2 of pattern, work cable panel between markers and work remaining stitches in Stockinette stitch, starting with Purl on next row. Work until piece measures 10" (9 ½", 9") in length.

Shape Armholes: Continuing center cables as established, work armhole shaping as for back. Continuing armhole and center cables, work even on 54 (60, 66) stitches until piece measures 15 ½" (or 1 ½" less than back).

Shape Neck: Continuing armhole cables, work first 20 (22, 24) stitches, drop old yarn, Slip center 14 (16, 18) stitches onto another stitch holder, attach

new yarn, work to end of row. Working each side of neck with its own separate yarn, bind off 4 stitches at each neck edge once, then decrease 1 stitch at each neck edge every other row 3 times. Work even on 13 (15, 17) stitches on each side until pieces measure same length as back. Bind off remaining stitches on each side loosely.

Sleeves: On smaller needles, cast on 28 (30, 32) stitches. Work in Knit 1, Purl 1 rib for 2 ½". Change to larger needles and work in Stockinette stitch, increasing 1 stitch on next row, then every sixth row 8 times more. Work even on 46 (48, 50) stitches until sleeve measures 17", ending with wrong-side row.

Shape Cap: Bind off 2 stitches at beginning of next 2 rows. Decrease 1 stitch at each edge as follows: *Row 1 (right side):* Knit 2, Slip Slip Knit, Knit to last 4 stitches, Knit 2 Together, Knit 2. *Row 2:* Purl across. Repeat these 2 rows until cap is 4". Bind off 2 stitches at beginning of next 4 rows. Bind off all remaining stitches loosely.

Finishing: Seam front and back at shoulders and underarms. Sew sleeve seams. Sew sleeve cap to shaped armhole at each side.

Neckband: With right side of work facing you, using circular needle and starting at center front, transfer 7 (8, 9) stitches from front holder to needle (use those stitches closest to right front of garment, leaving remaining stitches on holder). Attach yarn and Knit these 7 (8, 9) stitches, then pick up 12 stitches along right front neck edge to shoulder, Knit 24 (26, 28) stitches from back holder, pick up 11 stitches along left front neck edge, Knit remaining 7 (8, 9) stitches from front holder. Work back and forth on 61 (65, 69) stitches as follows: *Row 1 (wrong side):* Work in Knit 1, Purl 1 rib, ending with Knit 1. *Row 2:* Knit 2, work in Purl 1, Knit 1 rib to last stitch, Knit last stitch. Repeat these 2 rows for 1 ½", ending with right-side row. Bind off all stitches loosely in ribbing.

(Clockwise from left) This sweater has an inset sleeve;
the ribbing is modest at the wrist so it's not distracting;
this sweater is unbelievably comfortable and so
practical for my everyday life.

Project 4

SHERBET SCOOP NECK PULLOVER

This sweater was really enjoyable to make. It all started the day I walked into my local yarn shop and saw all these hot sherbet, almost Day-Glo, colors in cashmere. I could feel the tips of my fingers getting itchy—I just wanted to touch the yarn. As you know, cashmere is very expensive so I wouldn't make a coat out of it. But a small sweater? That I could afford. I chose a simple scoop neck pattern (no collar to worry about) and ¾-length sleeves. All that was left was choosing which color to use. I couldn't decide, so I thought: Why not do stripes? I used a lime green as the basic color, with other colors in between including red, turquoise, lavender, orange, and off-white.

(Above) The colors of the Sherbet Scoop Neck remind me of both spring and summer.

(Opposite) This is a cashmere and synthetic blend in colors yummy enough to eat.

Garment Sizes

32" (36", 40") to fit snuggly 32" (36", 40") body measurement at bust
Width of back at underarm: 16" (18", 20")
Length to shoulder: 18"
Sleeve length: 11"

Materials

Needles: 1 pair size 9 (5.5 mm) needles, 1 pair size 10 (6 mm) needles or size needed to obtain gauge
Yarn: The original yarn used in this project was a knitting-worsted weight cashmere blend in six colors: lime, main color (MC), and five different stripe colors (SC): red (also for ribbing), turquoise, orange, off-white, lavender.

Gauge

3.5 stitches per inch, 5.5 rows per inch, on larger needles

Basic Instructions

Back: On smaller needles, cast on 56 (64, 72) stitches with main color (MC) yarn. Work in Knit 1, Purl 1 rib for 1". Drop MC. Attach red and rib 3 rows. Cut red. With MC, continue in rib until ribbing measures 3 ¼" in length. Change to larger needles and attach stripe color (SC) yarn. With SC yarn, work in Stockinette stitch, working in stripe pattern of 4-row or 2-row stripes as desired with various SC yarns, working single row of MC between SC stripes. Work until piece measures 10" (9 ½", 9") in length.

Shape Armholes: Decrease 1 stitch at each side every other row 4 times. Work even on 48 (56, 64) stitches until piece measures 16 ½" in length, ending with wrong-side row.

Shape Neck: Work first 13 (15, 17) stitches, attach new yarn in same color. With new yarn bind off cen-

ter 22 (26, 30) stitches, work to end of row. Working each side with its separate yarn, bind off 3 (4, 5) stitches at each neck edge once, then decrease 1 stitch at each neck edge every other row twice. Work even on 8 (9, 10) stitches on each side until piece measures 18". Bind off remaining stitches on each side loosely.

Front: Work same as back to armhole shaping.

Shape Front Armholes: Decrease 1 stitch at each side every fourth row 4 times. Work even on 48 (56, 64) stitches until piece measure 14 ½" in length. Shape neck as for back. Then work even on 8 (9, 10) stitches on each side until piece measures same length as back. Bind off remaining stitches on each side loosely.

Sleeves: You can match stripes at underarm, or by adjusting sleeve cap stripe pattern to match yoke pattern at boldly colored (red) stripe as shown. To match stripes of sleeve and body at underarm, work ribbing and stripes as desired, working last 6 ¾" (6 ¼", 5 ¾") of sleeve in same stripe row pattern as you did for back and front to start of armholes. To work sleeve, on smaller needles and MC,

cast on 34 (36, 38) stitches. Work in Knit 1, Purl 1 rib for 1 ¼". Drop MC; attach SC. Change to larger needles and work in stripe pattern, increasing 1 stitch at each edge on next row, then every sixth row 5 (6, 7) times more. Work even on 46 (50, 54) stitches until sleeve measures 11", or length desired to underarm.

Shape Cap: Bind off 3 stitches at beginning of next 2 rows. Decrease 1 stitch at each edge on every other row until cap measures 4". Bind off 2 (3, 4) stitches at beginning of next 4 four rows, then bind off all remaining stitches loosely.

Finishing: Sew shoulder and underarm seams. Sew sleeve seams. Matching center of sleeve to shoulder seam, sew sleeve cap to shaped armhole on each side.

Neckband: With right side of work facing you, starting on left shoulder seam with MC and circular needle, pick up 90 (96, 102) stitches evenly spaced around neck edge. Join stitches and work in rounds on Knit 1, Purl 1 rib for 3 rounds. Bind off in ribbing.

(Left) I used green on the neckline, which is the "glue" throughout the sweater.

*(Clockwise from left) Notice how the stripes go from
4 rows of stitches on the bottom to 2 rows of stitches
at the top; when this sweater came out short, the experts
at my knitting shop showed me how to add on a few
more inches of ribbing at the bottom; stripes are difficult
to match when you sew your sweater together—
another reason to use a professional finisher.*

39

Project 5

REVERSIBLE BOATNECK PULLOVER

What inspires a sweater? Talent? Genius? Often, it's a need. For instance, the blue color for this sweater was influenced by a pair of my favorite shoes, a crisp and distinctive blue and white that nothing in my closet matched. The sweater's reversible style—with the front and the back interchangeable—was driven by the fact that I have a hard time determining which is the front and which is the back of other boatneck sweaters I own. In fact, I have to search for the label to determine which is the front. That got me thinking: Why not make it reversible on purpose? I started with a beige ribbon for both the front and the back, and then blended that ribbon with blue yarn for one side. I then blended it with a beige yarn for the other side. One sleeve is blue, and the other is beige. You can see I had fun with it. It's like having two sweaters in one.

(Above) The beige ribbon is used throughout. On one side, I mixed it with a blue twist by Katia, and on the other side I used the Katia twist in beige.

(Opposite) This reversible sweater can be worn with a beige front, as pictured here, or a blue front.

Garment Sizes

34" (36", 38", 40") to fit snuggly 34" (36", 38", 40") body measurement at bust
Width of back at underarm: 17" (18", 19", 20")
Length to shoulder: 18"
Sleeve length: 11"

Materials

Needles: 1 pair size 15 (10 mm) needles or size needed to obtain gauge, crochet hook size J (10 mm) for finishing
Yarn: The yarns used in this project were a ¼"-wide white ribbon (yarn A), and a loosely twisted knitting-worsted weight yarn in blue (yarn B) and in beige (yarn C). Yarns A and B were used together for blue sections and yarns A and C were used together for beige sections.

Gauge

2 stitches per inch, 3.5 rows per inch, on larger needles

Basic Instructions

Back: Cast on 36 (38, 40, 42) stitches with yarns A and B. With both yarns A and B, work in Stockinette stitch for 2". Cut B; attach C. With A and C, continue in Stockinette stitch 2" more. Cut yarn C; attach yarn B. With yarns A and B, work until piece measures 12" in total length.

Shape Armholes: Continuing with yarns A and B, bind off 3 stitches at beginning of next 2 rows. Decrease 1 stitch each arm edge every other row 3 times. Work even on 24 (26, 28, 30) stitches until piece measures 18" in length. Bind off all stitches loosely.

Straightening out Stripes

Check out the contrasting stripe just above the waist. On one side, it is neutral in contrast to the blue. On the other side, the stripe is blue in contrast to the neutral. You could, however, design your sweater so that the stripe is the same color on both sides. You decide. You design.

Having Fun in Reverse

This reversible sweater is fun. I had fun knitting it and I have fun wearing it. One day I can be in the mood to have the beige in front and the next day I may want the blue in front. It's especially convenient when I travel; one day I wear it with a blue pair of pants and the next day I may wear it with a pair of khakis. It just makes me smile.

Front: Work to correspond to back, but interchanging yarns C and B to make reverse color pattern.

First Sleeve: Loosely cast on 20 (22, 22, 24) stitches with yarns A and B. With both A and B, work in Stockinette stitch, increasing 1 stitch at each edge every sixth row 5 times. Work even on 30 (32, 32, 34) stitches until sleeve measures 11" or length desired to underarm.

Shape Cap: Bind off 3 stitches at beginning of next 2 rows. Decrease 1 stitch at each side on every other row until cap measures 3". Bind off 5 stitches at beginning of next 2 rows, then bind off remaining stitches loosely.

Second Sleeve: Loosely cast on 20 (22, 22, 24) stitches with yarns A and C. Work to correspond to first sleeve.

Finishing: Sew 1"-long shoulder seams at each arm edge, leaving wide neck opening. Sew underarm seams; sew sleeve seams. Matching center of sleeve to shoulder seam, sew sleeve cap to shaped armhole on each side.

Crocheted Edging: With yarn B only and using crochet hook, work row of single crochet around neck edge, then bottom edge of back, and cuff edge of first sleeve, crocheting stitches just loosely enough that edges lie flat without drawing in. Crochet row of single crochet around cuff edge of second sleeve and front, using yarn C only.

(Left) I like the flexibility of a boatneck sweater— I can wear it with a collared shirt, turtleneck, T-shirt, or by itself. The beauty of a reversible sweater is that the back is just as interesting as the front.

*(Clockwise from left) Here is where the blue side
meets the beige side at the shoulder line;
the ¾ sleeve has a crocheted edging; you can
see here the crocheted edge at the hem.*

Project 6

CARNIVAL PULLOVER

This sweater was so satisfying to design and knit, and to see it come alive. It started out when I fell in love with the colorful carnival ribbon yarn, which I used for the body. It turned out to be such a joy to work with, to feel and watch it grow in my hands. I wanted something different for the ribbing at the neck, wrists, and waist. I found a cotton-blend yarn that seemed to go well, but I couldn't decide if I wanted to use the purple color or the red. Both had flecks of other colors in them, and I finally surrendered to temptation and decided to use both yarns. You can see the alternating rows of purple and red on the ribbing. Somehow, with all these various elements, the sweater came together beautifully.

(Above) The red and purple yarns are called Samba by Stacy Charles, and the multicolor ribbon is called Wakaba by Noro.

(Opposite) Even when the weather is gloomy, the Carnival pullover cheers me up.

Garment Sizes
37 ½" (39", 41", 43 ½") to fit loosely 34" (36", 38", 40") body measurement at bust
Width of back at underarm: 19" (19 ¾", 20 ½", 21 ¾")
Length to shoulder: 18"
Sleeve length: 19"

Materials
Needles: 1 pair size 9 (5.5 mm) needles, 1 pair size 10 ½ (6.5 mm) needles or size needed to obtain gauge, 16"-long circular needle size 9 (5.5 mm) for neckband
Yarn: The original yarns used in this project were a novelty looped ribbon (yarn A) and a variegated sparkle strand blended with a fine cotton strand in purple (yarn B) and in red (yarn C). The ribbing edges were worked with double strands of B, alternated with C; the body and sleeves of the sweater were worked with a strand each of A and C.
Notions: 3 buttons, 2 shoulder pads

Gauge
3.3 stitches per inch, 6 rows per inch, on larger needles

Basic Instructions
Back: On smaller needles, cast on 60 (64, 68, 72) stitches with double strand of yarn B. Work in Knit 2, Purl 2 for 3 rows. Drop B. Attach double strand of C and work 2 more rib rows. Cut C. Then work 3 more rib rows with double B. Drop B. Attach double C and work 2 rows. Cut C. With double B, work 6 more rows. Cut B. Attach 1 strand of A and C. Change to larger needles and work with A and B, Knit across, increasing 2 (1, 1, 0) stitches evenly spaced across 62 (65, 69, 72) stitches. Starting with Purl row on wrong side, work in Stockinette stitch

until piece measures 18" in length. Bind off 17 (18, 19, 20) stitches loosely at beginning of next 2 rows. Slip remaining 28 (29, 31, 32) stitches onto stitch holder.

Front: Work same as back until piece measures 13" (or 5" less than back), ending with wrong-side row.

Shape Neck: Work first 28 (29, 31, 32) stitches, drop old yarn, attach another yarn A and B and with new yarns, bind off center 6 (7, 7, 8) stitches for base of placket; work to end of row. Working each side of neck with its own separate yarns, work even for 3 ½", then bind off 6 stitches at each neck edge once, then decrease 1 stitch at each neck edge every row 5 (5, 6, 6) times. Work even on 17 (18, 19, 20) stitches until piece measures same length as back. Bind off remaining stitches on each side loosely.

Sleeves: On smaller needles, loosely cast on 28 (28, 32, 32) stitches with double yarn B. Work in Knit 2, Purl 2 rib, alternating 2 rows of B and C until fourth C stripe is completed. Change to larger needles and work with 1 strand of A and B in Stockinette stitch, increasing 1 stitch at each edge on next row, then every eighth row 10 (11, 10, 11) times. Work even on 50 (52, 54, 56) stitches until sleeve measures 19". Bind off all stitches loosely.

Finishing:

For placket: With right side of work facing you, using double C and smaller needles, start at neck edge and pick up 18 stitches along vertical placket edge of left front. *Next row (wrong side):* Knit 2,

* Purl 2, Knit 2; repeat from * to end. *Following row:* Purl 2, * Knit 2, Purl 2; repeat from * to end. Repeat these 2 rows until 9 (9, 11, 11) rows of ribbing are completed. Bind off ribbing. On right front placket edge, start at bottom and pick up 18 stitches to neck edge with double C. Rib as for other side for 3 (3, 5, 5) rows, ending with a wrong-side row. *Next row (buttonhole row):* Purl 2, bind off next 2 Knit stitches (buttonhole made), Purl 2, Knit 2, bind off next 2 Purl stitches, Knit 2, Purl 2, bind off next 2 Knit stitches, Purl 2. On next row, keeping in rib as established, cast on 2 stitches over those bound off for each buttonhole. Continue in ribbing until total of 9 (9, 11, 11) ribbing rows are completed. Bind off in ribbing. Overlap bottom edges of placket ribbing with right side (with buttonholes) on top. Sew neatly in place to bound-off center stitches of front. Sew shoulder seams. Mark side edges of front and back 7 ½" (7 ¾", 8", 8 ¼") from shoulder seam. Matching center top of sleeve to shoulder seam, sew sleeve to each side between armhole markers. Sew sleeve and underarm seams.

Neckband: With right side of work facing you, using double C and circular needle, start at center top of right placket to pick up 66 (66, 70, 70) stitches evenly spaced around neck edge, including stitches from back holder, ending at center top of left placket. With double strand of B and C, work in Knit 2, Purl 2 rib as for left placket, working 6 rows with C, 2 rows with B, 4 rows with C, 2 rows with B, 4 rows with C. With C, bind off loosely in ribbing. Sew buttons to left placket, opposite buttonholes. Tack shoulder pads inside along shoulder seam.

(Left) The placket of red cotton yarn helps bring attention to the buttons.

(Clockwise from left) This sweater has a somewhat dressy yet sporty and casual look. I especially like to wear it with a green shirt and jeans; the stripes along the wrist are made of the same yarn as the waist ribbing, but are not as dramatic; notice how the ribbing contains none of the body yarn—this way, the purple cotton with the red cotton stripes stands out more.

47

Cardigans

Here is where you get to meet my wonderful cardigans. I'll share with you what inspired each sweater and my thought process as each sweater came into being. My hope is that you will understand how I've mixed yarns and altered basic patterns so that you may do the same to create the right sweater for you. As I mentioned in the first chapter, you might think these patterns are complicated, difficult, or even impossible. But that's just not the case. These sweaters are simple and quick, which is how I like my sweaters. Once you find a pattern that fits you well, know that you can make various sweaters with different yarns and different details that will flatter you. That takes a lot of the risk out of being your own sweater designer.

Project 1

IOWA GRAY MYLAR TWEED CARDIGAN

This sweater was inspired by a jazzy gray yarn I bought in Iowa. The yarn has specks of Mylar in it that give it sparkle. It was on sale in a knit shop there and I remember thinking, of course it's on sale. It was a bit wild for Iowa. I don't normally go for sparkly yarns, but since the skeins were deeply discounted, I couldn't resist. I took the yarn to my local knit shop and they worked up a pattern for me: a cardigan with a cowl collar. Because the yarn was dressy, I wanted to get a jacket look for nighttime. To me, this looks very nighttime, very holiday. Of all the sweaters I've knit, this is one of the most dressy.

(Above) I got this mohair yarn with Mylar flecks on sale at a shop in Iowa.

(Opposite) The knit shop worked up a cardigan pattern. I liked the pattern so much that I made several other sweaters with completely different looks.

Garment Sizes
36" (38", 40", 42") to fit 34" (36", 38", 40") body measurement at bust
Width of back at underarm: 18" (19", 20", 21")
Length to shoulder: 17"
Sleeve length: 17"

Materials
Needles: 1 pair size 9 (5.5 mm) needles, 1 pair size 10 ½ (6.5 mm) needles or size needed to obtain gauge, yarn needle for Kitchener stitch
Yarn: The original yarn used in this project was a medium-weight variegated gray mohair blended with a silver strand. This yarn was used throughout this sweater.
Notions: 2 shoulder pads

Gauge
3.5 stitches per inch, on larger needles

Pattern Stitch
Seed Stitch
To work on an even number of stitches.
Row 1: * Knit 1, Purl 1; repeat from * across.
Row 2: * Purl 1, Knit 1; repeat from * across.
Repeat these 2 rows for pattern.

Basic Instructions
Back: On smaller needles, cast on 64 (66, 70, 72) stitches. Work in Knit 1, Purl 1 rib for 1 ½". Change to larger needles. Work in Seed stitch until piece measures 10 ½" (10", 10", 9 ½") in length.

Shape Armholes: Keeping continuity of pattern stitch, bind off 3 stitches at beginning of next 2 rows. Decrease 1 stitch at each armhole edge every other row 4 times. Work even on 50 (52, 56, 58) stitches until piece measures 17" in length. Bind off 16 (17, 18, 19) stitches loosely at beginning of next 2 rows. Bind off remaining 18 (18, 20, 20) stitches for back neck.

Left Front: On smaller needles, cast on 43 (45, 45, 47) stitches. *Row 1 (right side):* Work in Knit 1, Purl 1 rib on next 34 (36, 36, 38) stitches, place marker on needle, Knit 9 for front border. Slipping marker on each row, work front border stitches in Garter stitch (Knit every row) and remaining stitches in ribbing as established until piece measures 1 ½" in length, ending with wrong-side row. Change to larger needles. *Next row:* Work in Seed stitch to marker, continue to work remaining stitches in Garter stitch until piece measures same as back to armhole shaping, ending with wrong-side row.

Shape Armhole and Collar: Starting at arm edge on next row, bind off 3 stitches, keeping continuity of pattern stitch, work in Seed stitch to last stitch before marker; add new marker, Knit 1, remove old marker, Knit to end of row. At front edge, there is now 1 more Garter stitch and there is 1 less stitch in Seed stitch section. Continue to decrease 1 stitch at arm edge every other row 4 (5, 4, 5) times more and at the same time at front edge on every third row, work 1 more stitch in Garter stitch and 1 less stitch in Seed stitch, moving markers as before, until there are 20 Garter stitches. Then work even on 36 (37, 38, 39) stitches until piece measures same length as back. At arm edge, bind off 16 (17, 18, 19) stitches once for shoulder. Work in Garter stitch on remaining 20 stitches for 5" (5", 5 ½", 5 ½") to form back section of collar. Slip all stitches onto stitch holder.

Right Front: On smaller needles, cast on 43 (45, 45, 47) stitches. *Row 1 (right side):* Knit 9 stitches for front border, place marker on needle, work in Knit 1, Purl 1 rib to end of row (arm edge). Work to correspond to left front, reversing shaping.

Sleeves: On smaller needles, loosely cast on 32 (34, 34, 36) stitches. Work in Knit 1, Purl 1 rib for 1 ½". Change to larger needles and work in Seed stitch, increasing 1 stitch every fourth row 12 times, keeping continuity of pattern as established. Work even on 56 (58, 58, 60) stitches until sleeve measures 17".

Shape Cap: Bind off 3 stitches at beginning of next 2 rows. Decrease 1 stitch at each edge every other row until cap measures 6 ½". Bind off 2 stitches at beginning of next 2 rows. Bind off all remaining stitches.

Finishing: Sew shoulder seams, leaving collar extensions free. Sew underarm seams. Sew sleeve seams. Matching center top of sleeve to shoulder seam, sew sleeve cap to shaped armhole on each side. Transfer back collar stitches to needles, using separate needle for each side. Weave stitches together with Kitchener stitch (or neatly sew adjoining stitches together on right side of work so it is hidden when collar is folded over). With joining at center back, neatly sew inner collar edge to back neck edge, easing to fit. Fold Garter stitch collar and front lapels outward to form cowl collar. Sew shoulder pads inside along shoulder seam.

(Left) The short length of the sweater adds to its dressiness.

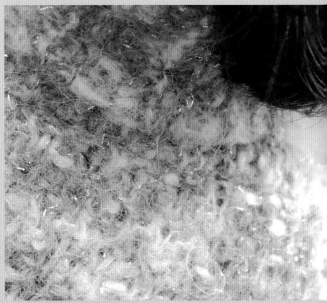

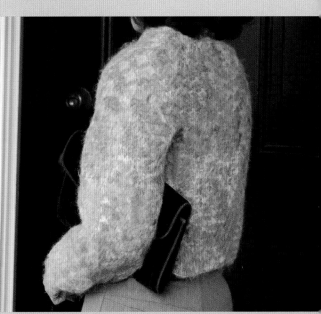

(Clockwise from left) This is a cowl collar; the back of the cowl collar is very elegant; the Iowa Gray Mylar Tweed is a simple sweater, but so dressy.

Project 2

GRAY CHENILLE CARDIGAN

For this sweater, I wanted to make another cowl collared cardigan. I'd gotten the pattern from my Iowa Gray Mylar Tweed sweater, but for this one I decided to try working with chenille, which I had never worked with before. When I say every stitch should be a kiss, this yarn makes it so. I chose this rich gray color and then decided on the style. The combination of this elegant yarn and the cardigan style gives it a jacket sort of look, somewhat on the dressy side. It looks great with a short flannel skirt or over a long skirt of some kind. I didn't want buttons, so something needs to be worn underneath. For the final touch, I chose a beautiful hand-dyed silk ribbon and, using a big, thick needle, wove the ribbon in and out, in and out, and then tied some bows.

(Above) There's only one yarn used here, a thick chenille in a color called Koala Gray.

(Opposite) The hand-dyed silk bows on my Gray Chenille sweater—one tied at the top, one tied at the bottom—produced a certain asymmetry that I find very appealing.

Garment Sizes
36" (38", 40", 42") to fit 34" (36", 38", 40") body measurement at bust
Width of back at underarm: 18" (19", 20", 21")
Length to shoulder: 18"
Sleeve length: 17"

Materials
Needles: 1 pair size 10 ½ (6.5 mm) needles or size needed to obtain gauge, large-eyed yarn needle for Kitchener stitch on collar, threading ribbons
Yarn: The original yarn used in this project was a bulky chenille in gray. This yarn was used throughout the sweater.
Notions: 3 yards of 3"-wide ribbon

Gauge
2 stitches per inch

Basic Instructions
Back: Cast on 36 (38, 40, 42) stitches. Work in Garter stitch (Knit every row) until piece measures 10" (10", 9 ½", 9 ½") in length.

Shape Armholes: Bind off 2 stitches at beginning of next 2 rows. Decrease 1 stitch at each armhole edge every other row twice. Work even on 28 (30, 32, 34) stitches until piece measures 18" in length. Bind off all stitches loosely.

Left Front: Cast on 18 (19, 20, 21) stitches. Work in Garter stitch until piece measures same as back to armhole shaping, ending with wrong-side row.

Forego the Ribbing

Notice that this sweater has no ribbing. That's because I wanted it to have a clean look. Normally, I like ribbing on a sweater, but here I wanted none of it. Why? I don't know; I just felt like it. That's what's nice about being your own sweater designer. You feel like doing something and you go with it. You decide. You design.

Shape Armhole: At beginning of next row, bind off 2 stitches once. At same edge (armhole edge), decrease 1 stitch every other row twice. Work even on 14 (15, 16, 17) stitches until armhole measures same as back.

Shape Shoulders and Back Collar: At arm edge, bind off 6 (7, 8, 9) stitches for shoulder, then work even on remaining 8 stitches for 3 ½" for back section of collar. Slip these 8 stitches onto stitch holder.

Right Front: Work to correspond to Left Front, reversing shaping.

Sleeves: Loosely cast on 16 (16, 18, 18) stitches. Work in Garter stitch, increasing 1 stitch at each edge every sixth row 8 times. Work even on 32 (32, 34, 34) stitches until sleeve measures 17", or length desired to underarm.

Shape Cap: Bind off 2 stitches at beginning of next 2 rows. Decrease 1 stitch at each edge on every other row times until cap measures 5". Bind off 2 stitches at beginning of next 2 rows. Bind off all remaining stitches loosely.

Finishing: Sew shoulder seams, leaving collar extensions free. Sew underarm sleeves. Sew sleeve seams. Matching center top of sleeve to shoulder seam, sew sleeve cap to shaped armhole on each side. Transfer collar stitches onto needles, using separate needle for each side. Weave stitches together with Kitchener stitch (or neatly sew adjoining stitches together on right side of work so it is hidden when collar is folded over). With joining at center back, neatly sew inner collar edge of back neatly to back neck edge, easing to fit. Fold back collar and front lapel edges to right side of garment as shown. To add ribbon trim, thread length up one front edge (about 2" in from front edge), around neck along lower edge of collar, and down opposite front edge. Cut off excess ribbon and secure ends on wrong side. Use excess ribbon to form 2 bows and attach 1 at neck and 1 at bottom on other side as shown.

(Left) A skirt, a blouse, my chenille sweater, and I'm off. This sweater is one of my more dressy projects, thanks to the rich yarn and tailored styling.

(Clockwise from left) As the perfect finishing touch, I wove the ribbon through the sweater and tied two bows, one on each side; I also opted for no ribbing at the waist; notice how there's no ribbing at the wrist—the yarn is so thick already, and I felt a ribbing would make it too bulky.

Project 3

BLACK MULTI-TWEED CARDIGAN

If I were showing you this sweater in person, I'd say, "Feel this! Feel how wonderful this is." I mixed a knubby multicolored novelty yarn with a mohair and a boucle to get this very thick sweater. Actually, this is the heaviest sweater I have. It is one warm sweater and it's luscious. It's like wearing a teddy bear suit or a polar bear suit. In a way, it's almost too heavy, considering the climate where I live. But it was fun to knit. The mix of yarns gives it a look different from any of my other sweaters. I like mixing yarns and seeing how they work together. As I often say, my idea of purgatory is knitting an all-black sweater, so this is as close as I will ever come to that.

(Above) This wonderfully thick sweater is a blend of a bulky black boucle, a black mohair, and a multi-colored novelty yarn.

(Opposite) The Black Multi-Tweed is a warm and heavy sweater and yet it's not over-sized and sloppy. With the right fit, you can be warm and chic at the same time.

Garment Sizes
34" (36", 38", 40") to fit snuggly 34" (36", 38", 40") body measurement at bust
Width of back at underarm: 17" (18", 19", 20")
Length to shoulder: 19"
Sleeve length: 17"

Materials
Needles: 1 pair size 13 (9 mm) needles, 1 pair size 15 (10 mm) needles or size needed to obtain gauge, yarn needle for Kitchener stitch
Yarn: The original yarns used in this project were a sportweight multicolored boucle (yarn A), a knitting-worsted weight black yarn (yarn B), and a black mohair (yarn C). All three yarns were used together throughout the sweater.

Gauge
1.9 stitches per inch, 3 rows per inch, on larger needles

Basic Instructions
Back: On smaller needles, cast on 34 (36, 38, 40) stitches with yarns A, B, and C. Work in Knit 1, Purl 1 rib for 1 ½". Change to larger needles and work in Stockinette stitch until piece measures 11" (10 ½", 10 ½", 10") in length, ending with wrong-side row.

Shape Armholes: Bind off 2 stitches at beginning of next 2 rows. Decrease 1 stitch at each armhole edge every other row twice. Work even on 26 (28, 30, 32) stitches until piece measures 19" in length. Bind off all stitches loosely.

Left Front: On smaller needles, cast on 22 (22, 24, 24) stitches with yarns A, B, and C. Work in Knit 1, Purl 1 rib for 1 ½". Change to larger needles. *Next row (right side):* Work in Stockinette stitch on next 17 (17, 18, 18) stitches, place marker on needle, work remaining 5 (5, 6, 6) stitches in Garter stitch (Knit every row) for front border. Work in patterns as now established until piece measures same as back to armhole shaping, ending with wrong-side row.

Shape Armhole and V-Neck: At beginning of next row, bind off 2 stitches (arm edge), work to last 2 stitches before marker, place new marker on needle, Knit 2 Together (neck decrease made), remove old marker, Knit to end of row. (*Note:* There are now 6 (6, 7, 7) stitches for front border.) At arm edge, decrease 1 stitch every other row 2 (1, 2, 1) times and at same time, work neck decrease of 1 stitch every fourth row 2 times more, transferring additional stitch to front border as before. Work even on 15 (16, 17, 18) stitches for 1 row. There are now 6 (7, 7, 8) stitches in Stockinette stitch and 9 (9, 10, 10) stitches in Garter stitch. Continue to work even in patterns as now established until piece measures same length as back. At arm edge, bind off 6 (7, 7, 8) stitches loosely for shoulder. Work even on remaining 9 (9, 10, 10) stitches in Garter stitch for 5" for back section of collar. Place stitches on holder.

Right Front: Work to correspond to Left Front, reversing shaping.

Sleeves: On smaller needles, loosely cast on 14 (16, 16, 18) stitches with yarns A, B, and C. Work in Knit 1, Purl 1 rib for 1 ½", increasing 1 stitch at end of last row 15 (17, 17, 19) stitches. Change to larger needles. Continuing with all three yarns, work in Stockinette stitch, increasing 1 stitch at each edge every fourth row 7 times. Work even on 29 (31, 31, 33) stitches until sleeve measures 17", or length desired, ending with wrong-side row.

Shape Cap: Bind off 2 stitches at beginning of next 2 rows. Decrease 1 stitch at each edge every other row until cap measure 3". Bind off 4 stitches at beginning of next 2 rows. Bind off all remaining stitches loosely.

Finishing: Sew shoulder seams, leaving collar extensions free. Sew underarm sleeves. Sew sleeve seams. Matching center top of sleeve to shoulder seam, sew sleeve cap to shaped armhole on each side. Transfer back collar stitches to needles, using separate needle for each side. Weave stitches together with Kitchener stitch (or neatly sew adjoining stitches together on right side of work so it is hidden when collar is folded over). With joining at center back, sew inner collar edge to back neck edge, easing to fit. Fold Garter stitch collar and front lapels outward to form cowl collar.

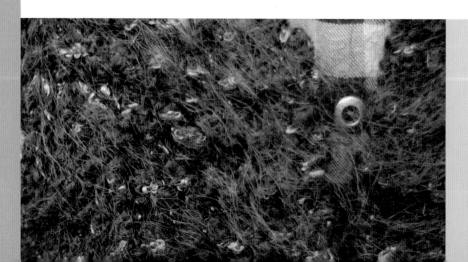

(Left) Few parkas can stand up to this sweater for warmth.

(Clockwise from left) This is a short sweater, but you could make yours longer by adding more rows of stitches; notice how the placket continues up around the neck; I didn't want anything fancy on the cuff, so I went with a rather modest ribbing.

61

Project 4

FLAG CARDIGAN

This is a very festive sweater, one that people notice and that gets them talking. So if you don't want to stand out in a crowd, you don't wear a sweater like this. If you do want to be noticed, however, this is the sweater for you. It's a very basic rounded neck cardigan, but because of the yarns I've chosen, it doesn't look plain at all. I call it my Flag sweater because the little pieces of fabric in the novelty yarn look like flags to me. I chose this yarn and then mixed it with another more substantial yarn to achieve the look I was after. Sometimes the flags would get stuck on the inside of the knitting fabric and I would take my needle and pull them through to the front. Of course, this changed the look of the particular row of knitting I was working on, and so it was fun to check out the pattern periodically. Whenever a sweater is fun to knit, I remember that good feeling every time I wear it.

(Above) Here's a unique combination: a fairly thick blue and white tweed wool, mixed with a mohair novelty yarn with colorful flags.

(Opposite) I can tone down the Flag cardigan with a denim shirt underneath, or kick it up with a silk shell.

Garment Sizes
36" (38", 40") to fit 34" (36", 38") body measurement at bust
Width of back at underarm: 18" (19", 20")
Length to shoulder: 19"
Sleeve length: 17"

Materials
Needles: 1 pair size 10 (6 mm) needles, 1 pair size 11 (8 mm) needles or size needed to obtain gauge
Yarn: The original yarns used in this project were a fuzzy, knitting-worsted weight blue tweed yarn (yarn A) and a novelty "flag" yarn (yarn B).
Notions: 5 buttons

Gauge
2.6 stitches per inch, 3.5 rows per inch, on larger needles

Basic Instructions
Back: On smaller needles, cast on 48 (50, 52) stitches with yarns A and B held together. Work in Knit 1, Purl 1 rib for 2". Change to larger needles. Using both A and B, work in Stockinette stitch until piece measures 11" (10 ½", 10") in length, ending with wrong-side row.

Shape Armholes: Bind off 3 stitches at beginning of next 2 rows. Decrease 1 stitch at each armhole edge every other row 3 times. Work even on 36 (38,

40) stitches until piece measures 19" in length. Bind off all stitches loosely.

Left Front: On smaller needles, cast on 24 (24, 26) stitches with A and B. Work in Knit 1, Purl 1 rib for 2", increasing 0 (1, 1) stitches at end of last row 24 (25, 27) stitches. Change to larger needles and work in Stockinette stitch until piece measures same as back to armhole shaping, ending with wrong-side row.

Shape Armhole: At beginning of next row, bind off 3 stitches once. At same edge (armhole edge), decrease 1 stitch every other row 3 times. Work even on 18 (19, 21) stitches until piece measures 17" (or 2" less than back), ending with wrong-side row.

Shape Neck: Starting at center front edge, bind off 5 stitches once, then 2 (2, 3) stitches once. At same edge, decrease 1 stitch every other row once. Work even on remaining 10 (11, 12) stitches until front measures same length as back. Bind off all stitches loosely.

Right Front: Work to correspond to Left Front, reversing shaping.

Sleeves: On smaller needles, loosely cast on 20 (20, 22) stitches with yarns A and B. Work in Knit 1, Purl 1 rib for 2", increasing 4 (5, 4) stitches evenly spaced across last row 24 (25, 26) stitches. Work in Stockinette stitch, increasing 1 stitch at each edge every sixth row 8 times. Work even on 40 (41, 42) stitches until sleeve measures 17", or length desired to underarm.

Shape Cap: Bind off 3 stitches at beginning of next 2 rows. Decrease 1 stitch at each edge on every other

row times until cap measures 5 ½". Bind off 5 stitches at beginning of next 2 rows. Bind off all remaining stitches loosely.

Finishing: Sew shoulder and underarm sleeves. Sew sleeve seams. Matching center top of sleeve to shoulder seam, sew sleeve cap to shaped armhole on each side.

Neckband: With right side of work facing you, using smaller needles and yarns A and B, pick up 65 (67, 69) stitches evenly spaced around neck edge. Work in Knit 1, Purl 1 rib for 1 ¼". Bind off in ribbing.

Front Bands: With right side of work facing you, using smaller needles and yarns A and B, start at neck edge to pick up 71 stitches evenly spaced along left front edge (including along neckband edge). *Next row (wrong side):* Purl 1, then work Knit 1, Purl 1 rib to end. Work in Knit 1, Purl 1 rib as established for 1 ¼". Bind off loosely in ribbing. Starting at bottom of sweater, pick up 71 stitches evenly spaced along right front edge to top of neckband. Establish ribbing same as for left band, and work until 3 rows of ribbing are completed. *Next row (right side):* Work buttonholes as follows: Keeping ribbing as established, rib 2 stitches, * Knit 3 Together, yarn over twice, (buttonhole made), rib next 13 stitches; repeat from * 3 times more, make another buttonhole, rib last 2 stitches. On following row, work in ribbing as established and at each buttonhole, Purl into first yarn over and Knit into second yarn over. Continue in ribbing until band is 1 ¼" wide. Bind off loosely in ribbing. Sew buttons to left band opposite buttonholes.

(Left) The gold in the buttons helps bring out the yellow in the flags.

(Clockwise from left) There is modest ribbing around the neck and packet; you can see the combination of striped wool yarn and the novelty flag—it's very unusual, but it works; the flags on this sweater are so much fun, both to knit with and to wear.

Project 5

COLORFUL TENNIS CARDIGAN

Before you ask, let me admit: No, I don't play tennis. But I like that crisp tennis look. If I ever get a ticket to Wimbledon, this will be the sweater to wear. My inspiration for this was a classic tennis sweater that would normally be a pullover. I wanted something I could wear over a T-shirt in the summer and just layer when it gets cooler. Then I fell in love with the crisp, multicolored cotton boucle. It just looked like spring and summer to me, with the red, yellow, and crisp white. Then I saw the contrasting dark blue yarn, which looked like denim. I knew it would go well with my favorite type of clothing: blue jeans.

(Above) The body of the sweater is made from this colorful cotton boucle. I also added a contrast yarn, of midnight blue cashmere and silk blend.

(Opposite) I added two blue stripes at the bottom, consisting of two rows each. You may prefer three rows of stripes or none at all.

Garment Sizes

36" (38", 40", 42") to fit 34" (36", 38", 40") body measurement at bust
Width of back at underarm: 18" (19", 20", 21")
Length to shoulder: 17 ½"
Sleeve length: 17"

Materials

Needles: 1 pair size 10 (6 mm) needles, 1 pair size 10 ½ (6.5 mm) needles or size needed to obtain gauge, 24"-long circular needle size 10 (6 mm) for front and neck trim
Yarn: The original yarns used in this project were a chunky multicolored cotton yarn (yarn A) and a denim blue yarn (yarn B).
Notions: 4 buttons

Gauge

8 stitches per 3 inches, 4 rows per inch, on larger needles

Basic Instructions

Back: On smaller straight needles, cast on 48 (52, 52, 56) stitches with yarn A. Work in Knit 2, Purl 2 rib for 2 rows. Drop A. Attach yarn B and work 2 rows in rib with B. Work 4 rows in rib with A, then 2 rows with B, increasing 0 (0, 2, 0) stitches on last row 48 (52, 54, 56) stitches. Cut B. Change to larger needles and with A only, work in Stockinette stitch until piece measures 11" (10 ¾", 10 ¾", 10 ½") in length, ending with wrong-side row.

Shape Armholes: Bind off 3 stitches at beginning of next 2 rows. Decrease 1 stitch at each armhole edge every other row 2 (3, 3, 3) times. Work even on 38 (40, 42, 44) stitches until piece measures 17" in length. Bind off all stitches loosely.

Left Front: On smaller needles, cast on 24 (24, 28, 28) stitches with A. Work in Knit 2, Purl 2 rib, changing colors as for back and increasing 0 (2, 0, 2)

Stripes That Slim

I chose the contrast color carefully to work best with this multi-colored cotton yarn. If I'd chosen red for the contrast stripes, it might have gotten lost. The same thing could be said of contrasting yellow stripes. Notice how the dark blue lines curving down the front are very slimming and lengthening to a figure. You decide. You design.

stitches on last row 24 (26, 28, 30) stitches. Change to larger needles and, with A only, work in Stockinette stitch until piece measures same as back to armhole shaping, ending with wrong-side row.

Shape Armhole and V-Neck: At beginning of next row (armhole edge), bind off 3 stitches once, Knit to last 2 stitches, Knit 2 Together (neck decrease). Continue in Stockinette stitch and at armhole edge, decrease 1 stitch every other row 2 (3, 4, 5) times more and at same time, work neck decrease of 1 stitch every third row 6 (6, 7, 7) times more. Work even on 12 (13, 13, 14) stitches until piece measures same length as back. Bind off all stitches loosely.

Right Front: Work to correspond to Left Front, reversing shaping.

Sleeves: On smaller needles, loosely cast on 20 (20, 24, 24) stitches with yarn A. Work in Knit 2, Purl 2 rib, changing colors as for back and increasing 4 (6, 2, 4) stitches evenly spaced across last row 24 (26, 26, 28) stitches. Change to larger needles and, using A only, work in Stockinette stitch, increasing 1 stitch at each edge every eighth row 6 times. Work even on 36 (38, 38, 40) stitches until sleeve measures 17", or length desired to underarm, ending with wrong-side row.

Shape Cap: Bind off 3 stitches at beginning of next 2 rows. Decrease 1 stitch at each edge on every other row times until cap measures 4". Bind off 5 (5, 6, 6) stitches at beginning of next 2 rows, then bind off all remaining stitches loosely.

Finishing: Sew shoulder and underarm sleeves. Sew sleeve seams. Matching center top of sleeve to shoulder seam, sew sleeve cap to shaped armhole on each side.

Front and Neck Trim: With right side of work facing you, using circular needle and yarn A, start at lower right front edge to pick up 74 (74, 75, 75) stitches evenly spaced along right front edge to shoulder, 18 (18, 20, 20) stitches along back neck edge, and 74 (74, 75, 75) stitches evenly spaced down left front edge to bottom edge. Work ribbing on 166 (166, 170, 170) stitches as follows: *Row 1 (wrong side):* Purl 2, work in Knit 2, Purl 2 rib with A; change to B next row (right-side buttonhole row): Knit 2, Purl 2, * yarn over, Knit 2 Together (buttonhole made), Purl 2, Knit 2, Purl 2, Knit 2, Purl 2; repeat from * twice more, yarn over, Knit 2 Together, then continue in rib as established to end. Rib 1 more row with B. Change to A and rib 1 row. With A bind off all stitches loosely. Sew buttons to left front opposite buttonholes.

(Left) Because red is my favorite color, I wear this sweater a lot.

*(Clockwise from left) The vertical line of blue up
the front is flattering since it lengthens the look of the
body; this double stripe with contrasting color
makes a strong horizontal line at the waist;
a contrasting trim runs up around the neck.*

Project 6

SCOTLAND CARDIGAN

This sweater was inspired by the gray and brown yarn I found on a trip to Scotland. The two tones were chosen simply because I couldn't decide which yarn I liked better—the light gray background or the dark gray background. They both had the same brown in them and both were equally appealing to me. Ultimately, I decided to use the darker gray for the body of the long cardigan, and the light gray for the trim. Generally speaking, it's more slimming if the darker tone is on the body rather than the lighter tone.

(Above) I used a brown wool tweed for the body, a gray wool tweed for the sleeves, and alternated the trim throughout.

(Opposite) I made this sweater in Scotland. Here I'm pulling a potato from my garden.

Garment Sizes
40" (42", 44") to fit loosely 34" (36", 38") body measurement at bust
Width of back at underarm: 20" (21", 22")
Length to shoulder: 26"
Sleeve length: 17"

Materials
Needles: 1 pair size 10 (6 mm) needles, 1 pair size 11 (8 mm) needles or size needed to obtain gauge
Yarn: The original yarns used in this project were a heavyweight dark brown woolen tweed (yarn A) and a heavyweight gray woolen tweed with flecks of tan (yarn B). Yarn A was used for the body of the sweater, and yarn B for the sleeves and trim.
Notions: 6 buttons

Gauge
2.5 stitches per inch, 3.5 rows per inch, on larger needles

Basic Instructions
Back: On smaller needles, cast on 52 (52, 56) stitches with yarn A. Work in Knit 2, Purl 2 rib for 4 rows. Drop A. Attach yarn B and rib 2 rows. Cut B. With A, rib 2 more rows, increasing 0 (2, 0) stitches on last row 52 (54, 56) stitches. Change to larger needles. With A, work in Stockinette stitch until piece measures 17" (16 ½", 16") in length.

Shape Armholes: Decrease 1 stitch at each arm edge every other row 8 times. Work even on 36 (38, 40) stitches until piece measures 26" in length. Bind off all stitches loosely.

Pocket Linings: On larger needles, using yarn A, cast on 12 stitches. Work even in Stockinette stitch for 4". Slip all 12 stitches on stitch holder. Make second pocket lining in same manner.

Left Front: On smaller needles, cast on 24 stitches for all sizes with B. Work in Knit 2, Purl 2 rib, changing colors as for back and increasing 0 (1, 2) stitches on last row 24 (25, 26) stitches. Change to

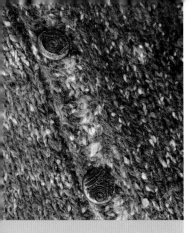

(Above) The personality of a sweater can be determined by the buttons.

larger needles and with A, work in Stockinette stitch until piece measures 8" in length, ending with wrong-side row. *Next row (right side):* Work pocket opening as follows: Starting at arm edge, Knit 6 (7, 8), Slip next 12 stitches to another stitch holder, transfer 12 stitches of one pocket lining to left needle with right side of work facing you, Knit across lining stitches, then Knit remaining 6 stitches of front. Work even on 24 (25, 26) stitches until piece measure same length as back to armhole shaping, ending with wrong-side row.

Shape Armhole: At arm edge, decrease 1 stitch every other row 8 times. Work even on 16 (17, 18) stitches until piece measures 21" (or 5" less than back), ending with right-side row.

Shape Neck: Starting at neck edge, bind off 5 stitches once, then 2 stitches once. At same edge decrease 1 stitch every other row twice. Work even on remaining 7 (8, 9) stitches until piece measures same length as back. Bind off remaining stitches on each side loosely.

Right Front: Work same as Left Front to pocket opening. Starting at front edge, Knit 6, Slip next 12 stitches to stitch holder, Knit 12 stitches of remaining pocket lining, then Knit remaining 6 (7, 8) stitches of front. Complete to correspond to Left Front, reversing shaping.

Sleeves: On smaller needles, loosely cast on 24 stitches for all sizes with yarn B. Work in Knit 2, Purl 2 ribbing for 4 rows, then rib 2 rows with yarn A, 2 rows with yarn B, increasing 0 (2, 4) stitches on last row 24 (26, 28) stitches. Change to larger needles and, continuing with B, work in Stockinette stitch, increasing 1 stitch at each edge every fifth row 8 times. Work even on 40 (42, 44) stitches until sleeve measures 17", or length desired to underarm, ending with wrong-side row.

Shape Cap: Bind off 3 stitches at beginning of next 2 rows. Decrease 1 stitch at each edge on every

other row times until cap measures 6". Bind off all remaining stitches loosely.

Finishing: Transfer 12 pocket opening stitches on one front from holder to larger needle. *Row 1 (right side):* With B, Knit and increase 1 stitch in first stitch, * Purl 2, Knit 2; repeat from * once more, Purl 2, Knit and increase 1 stitch in last stitch (14 stitches). *Next row:* Purl 2, work Knit 2, Purl 2 rib across. Bind off in ribbing. Repeat pocket trim on other front. Sew each pocket lining in place on wrong side of fronts. Sew side edges of pocket trim just made in place on right side of fronts. Sew shoulder and underarm sleeves. Sew sleeve seams. Matching center top of sleeve to shoulder seam, sew sleeve cap to shaped armhole on each side.

Collar: With wrong side of work facing you, using yarn A and smaller needles, pick up 54 stitches around neck edge. *Next row (wrong side of collar):* Purl 2, work in Knit 2, Purl 2 rib to end. Rib as established for 2". Change to larger needle and continue until ribbing measures 3 ½" in length, ending with wrong-side row. Work 2 rows with B, then 3 more rows with A. Bind off all stitches loosely in ribbing.

Front Bands: With right side of work facing you, using smaller needles and yarn A, start at neck edge and pick up 74 stitches evenly spaced along left front edge to bottom. *Next row (wrong side):* Purl 2, work in Knit 2, Purl 2 rib to end. With yarn B, work 2 more rib rows as established. With A, rib 1 row, then bind off all stitches in ribbing. Mark placement for 6 buttons on front band, with first button 1" from bottom, top button 1" below neck edge, and others spaced evenly between. Starting at bottom, pick up 74 stitches evenly spaced along right front edge to neck. Work in rib as for left front, changing colors and working buttonhole on third row (right side of work) opposite each marker by making yarn over, then working 2 stitches together (Knit or Purl as needed). Complete front band. Sew buttons to left front opposite buttonholes. Fold collar outward as shown.

(Clockwise from left) This combination of yarns actually works better for me than the combination I used in the Red Scotland sweater that follows; the subtle stripe draws attention to the collar; here is another subtle stripe on the sleeve, this time dark brown on a gray sleeve.

Project 7

RED-SLEEVE SCOTLAND CARDIGAN

I made this sweater immediately after I made my Scotland sweater because I really liked how that one turned out. Up until then, I had never made a longer sweater, and I really liked how it felt. It was wintertime and I was ready for another long project to warm my lap. This is almost exactly the same pattern as the Scotland, except there are more stripes on the arms of the contrasting color. For the body, I mixed a gray tweed yarn with a white yarn, and for the contrast I mixed the same white with a red.

(Above) For this sweater I used four yarns: a red wool, a black-and-white striped wool, a white cotton boucle, and a white mohair.

(Opposite) I included thin contrasting stripes on the sleeves of this sweater.

Garment Sizes
40" (42", 44") to fit loosely 34" (36", 38") body measurement at bust
Width of back at underarm: 20" (21", 22")
Length to shoulder: 26"
Sleeve length: 17"

Materials
Needles: 1 pair size 10 (6 mm) needles, 1 pair size 11 (8 mm) needles or size needed to obtain gauge
Yarn: The original yarns used in this project were a heavyweight gray tweed formed by a blend of a black-and-white strand and a white mohair-type strand (yarn A), and a heavyweight red tweed formed by a blend of a thin red woolen strand, 2 red mohair-type strands, and a white nubby strand (yarn B). Yarn A is used for the body of the sweater, and yarn B for the sleeves, stripes, and trim.
Notions: 6 buttons, shoulder pads

Gauge
2.5 stitches per inch, 3.5 rows per inch, on larger needles

Basic Instructions
Back: On smaller needles, cast on 52 (52, 56) stitches with yarn A. Work in Knit 2, Purl 2 rib for 2 rows. Drop A. Attach B and rib 2 rows. Cut B. Change to larger needles. Continuing with B, Knit across, increasing 0 (2, 0) stitches on last row 52 (54, 56) stitches. Starting with Purl row, work in Stockinette stitch until piece measures 17" (16 ½", 16") in length.

Shape Armholes: Decrease 1 stitch at each arm edge every other row 8 times. Work even on 36 (38, 40) stitches until piece measures 26" in length. Bind off all stitches loosely.

Pocket Linings: On larger needles, using yarn A, cast on 12 stitches. Work even in Stockinette stitch for 4". Slip all 12 stitches to stitch holder.

Left Front: On smaller needles, cast on 24 stitches for all sizes with yarn B. Work in Knit 2, Purl 2 rib, changing colors as for back and increasing 0 (1, 2) stitches on last row 24 (25, 26) stitches. Change to larger needles and with A, work in Stockinette stitch

until piece measures 8", ending with wrong-side row. *Next row (right side):* Work pocket opening as follows: Starting at arm edge, Knit 6 (7, 8), Slip next 12 stitches to another stitch holder, transfer 12 stitches of pocket lining to left needle with right side of work facing you, Knit across lining stitches, then Knit remaining 6 stitches of front. Work even on 24 (25, 26) stitches until piece measures same length as back to armhole shaping, ending with wrong-side row.

Shape Armhole: At arm edge, decrease 1 stitch every other row 8 times. Work even on 16 (17, 18) stitches until piece measures 21" (or 5" less than back), ending with right-side row.

Shape Neck: Starting at neck edge, bind off 5 stitches once, then 2 stitches once. At same edge decrease 1 stitch every other row twice. Work even on remaining 7 (8, 9) stitches until piece measures same length as back. Bind off remaining stitches on each side loosely.

Right Front: Work same as Left Front to pocket opening. Starting at front edge, Knit 6, Slip next 12 stitches to stitch holder, Knit 12 stitches of second pocket lining, then Knit remaining 6 (7, 8) stitches of front. Complete to correspond to Left Front, reversing shaping.

Sleeves: On smaller needles, loosely cast on 24 stitches for all sizes with B. Work in Knit 2, Purl 2 ribbing for 4 rows, then rib 2 rows with A, 2 rows with B, increasing 0 (2, 4) stitches on last row 24 (26, 28) stitches. Change to larger needles and, continuing with B, work in Stockinette stitch, increasing 1 stitch at each edge every fifth row 8 times. At same time work stripes as follows: When sleeve measures 3 ½", work 2 rows with A, then 8 rows with B, 2 rows with A, 14 rows with B, 2 rows with A, complete sleeve with B. Work even on 40 (42, 44) stitches until sleeve measures 17", or length desired to underarm, ending with wrong-side row.

Shape Cap: Bind off 3 stitches at beginning of next 2 rows. Decrease 1 stitch at each edge on every other row times until cap measures 5". Bind off all remaining stitches loosely.

Finishing: Transfer 12 pocket opening stitches on front from holder to larger needle. *Row 1 (right side):* With B, Knit and increase 1 stitch in first stitch, * Purl 2, Knit 2; repeat from * once more, Purl 2, Knit, and increase 1 stitch in last stitch (14 stitches). *Next row:* Purl 2, work Knit 2, Purl 2 rib across. Bind off in ribbing. Repeat pocket trim on other front. Sew each pocket lining in place on wrong side of fronts. Sew side edges of pocket trim just made in place on right side of fronts. Sew shoulder and underarm sleeves. Sew sleeve seams. Matching center top of sleeve to shoulder seam, sew sleeve cap to shaped armhole on each side.

Front Bands: With right side of work facing you, using smaller needles and yarn B, start at neck edge and pick up 78 stitches evenly spaced along left front edge to bottom. *Next row (wrong side):* Purl 2, work in Knit 2, Purl 2 rib to end. With yarn A, work 5 more rib rows as established, then bind off all stitches in ribbing. Mark placement for 6 buttons on front band, with first button 1" from bottom, top button 1" below neck edge, and others spaced evenly between. Starting at bottom, pick up 78 stitches evenly spaced along right front edge to neck. Work in rib as for left front, changing colors and working buttonhole on third row (right side of work) opposite each marker by making yarn over, then working 2 stitches together (Knit or Purl as needed). Complete front band. Sew buttons to left front opposite buttonholes.

Stand-Up Collar: With right side of work facing you, using yarn B and smaller needles, pick up 46 stitches around neck edge, starting and ending at center top of front bands. *Next row (wrong side of collar):* Purl 2, work in Knit 2, Purl 2 rib to end. Rib as established for 2 ¾". Bind off all stitches loosely in ribbing. Sew buttons to left front band, opposite buttonholes. Sew shoulder pads inside sweater along shoulder seam.

(Clockwise from left) With this sweater, the light gray body is perhaps too strikingly different from the red arms; contrasting stripes add interest to the sleeves; the red is used for contrast on the pocket.

Project 8

LONG RED RIBBON CARDIGAN

Unlike most of my sweaters, this one is not a blend of yarns. It's made of a rayon-type ribbon, kind of like a bias tape, and nothing else. I decided to include cables on it so it wouldn't be too boring to make. The motivation for this sweater was that I wanted to give myself the experience of using this type of yarn, and the thing was, it was really fun to knit with. I get good use out of this sweater, wearing it with jeans or even workout clothes.

(Above) There's only one yarn in this sweater, a red ribbon.

(Opposite) I wanted to try ribbon yarn so I made this long cardigan in my favorite color.

Garment Sizes
36" (38", 40", 42") to fit 34" (36", 38", 40") body measurement at bust
Width of back at underarm: 18" (19", 20", 21")
Length to shoulder: 25"
Sleeve length: 17"

Materials
Needles: 1 pair size 10 ½ (6.5 mm) needles, 1 pair size 11 (8 mm) needles or size needed to obtain gauge, cable needle, 24"-long circular needle size 10 ½ (6.5 mm) for front and neck trim
Yarn: The original yarn used in this project was a ⅜"-wide ribbon. A single strand of the ribbon was used throughout the sweater.
Notions: 3 or more buttons as desired

Gauge
4 stitches per inch, 5 rows per inch, on larger needles

Cable Panel
Worked on 14 stitches.
Row 1 (right side): Purl 3, Knit 8, Purl 3

Row 2 and all wrong-side rows: Knit 3, Purl 8, Knit 3
Row 3 (cable twist): Purl 3, Slip 4 stitches to cable needle and hold in front of work, Knit 4, Knit 4 from cable needle, Purl 3
Row 5: Repeat Row 1
Row 7: Repeat Row 1
Row 8: Repeat Row 8
Repeat these 8 rows for cable panel.

Basic Instructions
Back: On smaller needles, cast on 72 (76, 80, 84) stitches. Work in Knit 1, Purl 1 rib for 1 ½". Change to larger needles and work in Stockinette stitch until piece measures 17" (16 ¾", 16 ½", 16 ¼") in length.

Shape Armholes: Bind off 3 stitches at beginning of next 2 rows. Decrease 1 stitch at each armhole edge every other row 4 times. Work even on 58 (62, 66, 70) stitches until piece measures 25" in length. Bind off 17 (19, 20, 22) stitches loosely, work center 24 (24, 26, 26) stitches and place them on stitch holder. Bind off remaining stitches loosely.

Different types of yarns have different qualities of resiliency, or ability to bounce back. Wool is the queen of yarns for its ability to keep its shape (if you treat it right and don't put it in the dryer, that is). Cotton is less resilient and more likely to stretch. Ribbon yarn, used by itself, is the least resilient. If you make a garment out of this ribbon, be sure to store it folded up, rather than hanging it, or the piece will have a tendency to grow over time.

Left Front: On smaller needles, cast on 38 (40, 42, 44) stitches. Work in Knit 1, Purl 1 rib for 1 ½", increasing 4 stitches evenly spaced across last row 42 (44, 46, 48) stitches. Change to larger needles. *Next row (right side):* Knit 14 (15, 16, 17), place marker on needle, work row 1 of cable panel on next 14 stitches, place another marker on needle, Knit 14 (15, 16, 17). Continue to work cable panel between markers and remaining stitches in Stockinette stitch until piece measures 15" in length.

Shape V-Neck and Armholes: At center front edge (neck edge), decrease 1 stitch on next row, then every third row 13 (14, 15, 16) times more, continuing cable as established and at same time, when piece measures same as back to armhole shaping, at arm edge, bind off 3 stitches once. At same edge decrease 1 stitch every other row 6 (5, 5, 5) times. Work even on 19 (21, 22, 23) stitches until piece measures same as back. Bind off all remaining stitches.

Right Front: Work to correspond to Left Front, reversing all shaping.

Sleeves: On smaller needles, loosely cast on 32 (34, 36, 38) stitches. Work in Knit 1, Purl 1 rib for 1 ½". Change to larger needles and work in Stockinette stitch, increasing 1 stitch at each edge on next row, then every eighth row 8 times more. Work even on 50 (52, 54, 56) stitches until sleeve measures 17", or length desired to underarm.

Shape Cap: Bind off 3 stitches at beginning of next 2 rows. Decrease 1 stitch at each edge until cap measures 4". Bind off 5 stitches at beginning of next 4 rows, then bind off all remaining stitches loosely.

Finishing: Leaving center back 24 (24, 26, 26) stitches free for back neck, sew shoulder seams, easing back shoulder to fit front shoulder (which has more stitches because of cable). Sew underarm seams. Sew sleeve seams. Matching center top of sleeve to shoulder seam, sew sleeve cap to shaped armhole on each side.

Front and Neck Trim: With right side of work facing you, using circular needle, start at lower right front edge and pick up 91 stitches evenly spaced along right front edge to shoulder, Knit 24 (24, 26, 26) stitches from holder, pick up 90 stitches evenly spaced along left front edge from shoulder to bottom. *Work as follows:* Row 1 (wrong side): Purl 1, work in Knit 1, Purl 1 rib to end. Plan placement for 3 or more buttons evenly spaced apart on Left Front as desired. With safety pins, mark corresponding place on Right Front for buttonholes. *Next row (right-side buttonhole row):* Work in Knit 1, Purl 1 rib as established and make buttonhole at each safety pin marker as follows: Yarn over, work 2 stitches together (Knit or Purl as needed), then complete row, ending with Knit 1. Work 2 more rib rows. Bind off loosely in ribbing. Sew buttons to Left Front opposite buttonholes.

(Left) These buttons are very simple—I wasn't looking to make a statement.

(Clockwise from left) If you tend to wear tight pants for your workout, a long sweater can be more flattering; I chose a standard Knit 1, Purl 1 ribbing at the wrist; this is a very basic everyday sweater, and the cable adds a bit of interest.

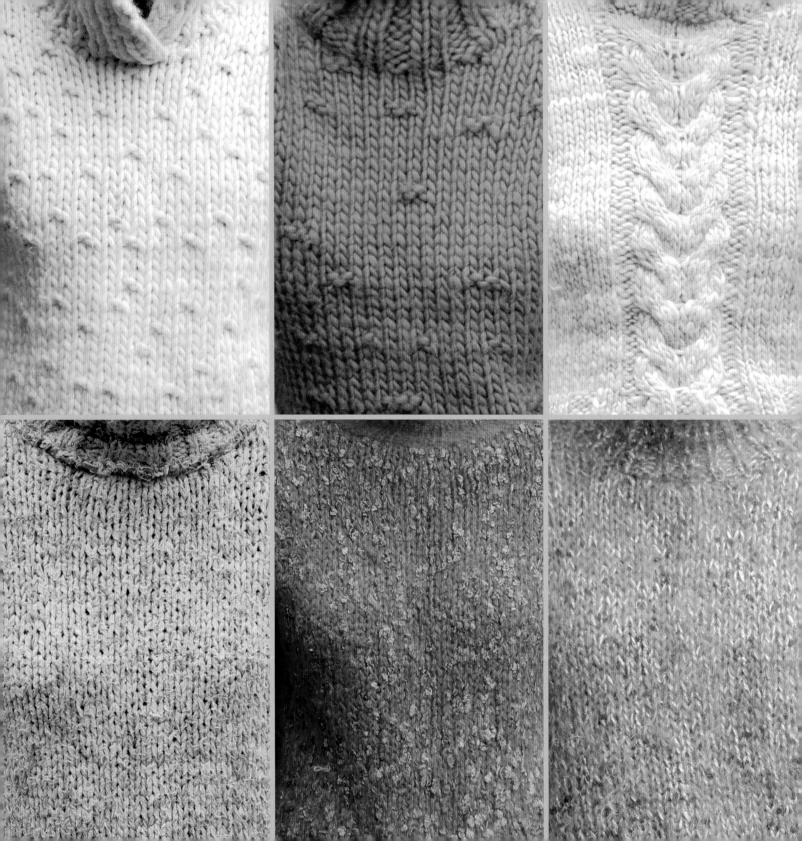

Turtlenecks

For a while I was on a turtleneck kick, and this chapter shows you the fruits of that labor, that obsession, if you will. I like to be warm, I like to feel zipped up, so turtlenecks work for me. I've got a basic turtleneck pattern that I've used many, many times. I know how long I like the body, and how long I like the arms. This chapter is a graphic study of how you can take one basic pattern and alter the yarns and details to create many different looks. Some are showy, others are just plain comfortable—yet stylish. And never, ever sloppy. The joy of a wonderful pattern is being able to alter it to create interest, to have fun, and to design new and unique looks in a silhouette that you know works for you.

Turtleneck Projects:

1. Random Purl Turtlenecks
2. Pink and Purple Wide Rib
3. Palomino
4. Denim Turtle with Twisted Braid
5. Red Tweed with Contrasting Neck and Aqua Silver

Project 1

RANDOM PURL TURTLENECKS

These three sweaters, all made with what I call a Random Purl stitch pattern, illustrate a really important lesson in this book, which is to take a basic pattern that works for you and alter it. With these sweaters, I started out with two things going for me: a turtleneck pattern that fits and flatters, and a wonderfully thick wool. I fell in love with this wool. I was crazy for this wool. Then, by adding two more of my own creative touches, I've managed to make three sweaters that look and wear quite differently. As you know, most ribbing is a Knit 1, Purl 1 (or Knit 2, Purl 2) within the same row, while the body of most sweaters is a row of Knit followed by a row of Purl. With these sweaters, I've managed to shake up both the standard ribbing and the standard Stockinette stitch with no great talent on my part, but with a sense of fun and adventure.

Garment Sizes

36" (38", 40", 42") to fit snugly 34" (36", 38", 40") body measurement at bust
Width of back at underarm: 18" (19", 20", 21")
Length to shoulder: 20"
Sleeve length: 18"

Materials

Needles: 1 pair size 17 (12.75 mm) needles or size needed to obtain gauge, 16"-long circular needle size 11 (8 mm) for turtleneck
Yarn: The original yarn used in this project was a very bulky wool yarn that produces a firm texture with little stretch. If you prefer a more relaxed fit, knit a larger size sweater than usual for you. This yarn was used for the entire sweater.

Gauge

2 stitches per inch, 3 rows per inch, on larger needles

Basic Instructions

Note: The random pattern for this sweater has single Purl stitches scattered on Stockinette stitch ground, usually with at least 1" between surrounding Purl bumps.

Back: On straight needles, cast on 36 (38, 40, 42) stitches. Work in Knit 1, Purl 1 rib for 3". Now work in random Purl pattern on Stockinette stitch until piece measures 20" in length. Bind off all stitches loosely.

Front: Work same as back until piece measures 17" (or 2 ½" less than back), ending with wrong-side row.

Shape Neck: Work first 14 (15, 15, 16) stitches, drop old yarn, attach new yarn and with new yarn, bind off center 8 (8, 10, 10) stitches, work to end of row. Working each side of neck with its own separate yarn, decrease 1 stitch at each neck edge every other row 2 (3, 2, 3) times. Work even on 12 (13, 13, 13) stitches until piece measures same length as back. Bind off remaining stitches on each side loosely.

Sleeves: On straight needles, loosely cast on 16 (16, 18, 18) stitches. Work in Knit 1, Purl 1 rib for 4". Work in random Purl pattern and increase 1 stitch at each edge on next row, then every 8th (6th, 8th, 6th) row 5 (6, 5, 6) times more. Work even on 28 (30, 30, 32) stitches until sleeve measures 18" or length desired. Bind off all stitches loosely.

Finishing: Sew shoulder seams. Mark side edges of front and back 7" (7 ½", 7 ½", 8") from shoulder seams. Matching center of sleeve to shoulder seam, sew top edge of sleeve to sweater between side armhole markers. Sew sleeve and underarm seams.

Split Turtleneck: With right side of work facing you, starting at 3rd (3rd, 4th, 4th) bound-off stitch of center front neck, pick up 1 stitch in front loop of next 6 (6, 7, 7) bound-off stitches, then pick up 38 (38, 39, 41) stitches around neck edge, ending in first 2 (2, 3, 3) bound-off stitches at front neck; then reaching needle behind beginning stitches, pick up stitch in back loop of next 3 stitches to form overlap 47 (47, 49, 51) stitches. *Next row (wrong side):* Purl 1, work Knit 1, Purl 1 rib to end. Work back and forth in rib as established for 3 ½". Bind off in ribbing.

(Left) This is a firewood-carrying sweater. I especially like wearing it in the fall.

(Clockwise from left) These random Purl stitches give the same spirit of a fisherman's sweater, but with much less work; notice how the collar is slit, and one side crosses over; the cuff ribbing is Knit 1, Purl 1.

(From top) With this sweater, I went with a crew neck;
the waist ribbing is very fun—Knit 5, Purl 2;
the ribbing on this sleeve is quite deep.

(Right) The random purls on this sweater are more
numerous than on the green or beige sweater.

(From top) The high collar gives this sweater a custom look; the deep ribbing is definitely a design element; I knit a Purl 5, Knit 2 ribbing on the cuff and hem.

(Left) A wide ribbing defines this sweater.

Project 2

PINK AND PURPLE WIDE RIB TURTLENECK

With this sweater, I chose this pink and purple yarn and then decided to knit

a ribbing over the whole sweater.

Garment Sizes

36" (38", 40", 42") to fit 34" (36", 38", 40")
body measurement at bust
Width of back at underarm: 18" (19", 20", 21")
Length to shoulder: 18"
Sleeve length: 17"

Materials

Needles: 1 pair size 17 (12.75 mm) needles or size
needed to obtain gauge, 16"-long circular needle
size 11 (8 mm) for neckband
Yarn: The original yarn used in this project was a
heavyweight thick and thin wool, variegated purple
and pink. This yarn was used throughout the sweater.

Gauge

10 stitches per 3 inches, 4 rows per inch, in rib
pattern on straight needles

Basic Instructions

Back: On straight needles, cast on 50 (54, 58, 62)
stitches with yarn. Work in Knit 1, Purl 1 rib for
2 ½", increasing 10 stitches evenly spaced across last
row 60 (64, 68, 72) stitches. *Work in rib pattern as
follows:* Row 1 (right side): Purl 0 (2, 4, 6), * Knit 6,
Purl 6; repeat from *, ending Knit 0 (2, 4, 6). Repeat
this row for pattern. Work until piece measures 18"
in length. Bind off 18 (19, 21, 22) stitches loosely at
beginning of next 2 rows. Slip remaining 24 (26, 26,
28) stitches on stitch holder for back neck.

Front: Work same as back until piece measures 16"
(or 2" less than back), ending with wrong-side row.

Shape Neck: Work first 24 (25, 27, 28) stitches,

drop old yarn, slip center 12 (14, 14, 16) stitches
onto stitch holder for center front neck, attach new
yarn and with new yarn, work to end of row.
Working each side of neck with its own separate
yarns, bind off 4 stitches at each neck edge once,
then decrease 1 stitch at each neck edge every row
twice. Work even on 18 (19, 21, 22) stitches until
piece measures same length as back. Bind off
remaining stitches on each side loosely.

Sleeves: On straight needles, loosely cast on 26 (28,
28, 30) stitches. Work in Knit1, Purl 1 rib for 2 ½",
increasing 6 stitches evenly spaced across last row 32
(34, 34, 36) stitches. *Establish rib pattern as follows:*
Next row (right side): Purl 1 (2, 2, 3), * Knit 6, Purl 6;
repeat from * once more, Knit 6, Purl 1 (2, 2, 3). Work
in pattern as established for 5 more rows. Keeping
continuity of pattern, increase 1 stitch at each edge on
next row, then every 6th row 6 times more, working
added stitches in pattern. Work even on 46 (48, 48,
50) stitches until sleeve measures 17", or length
desired to underarm. Bind off all stitches loosely.

Finishing: Sew shoulder seams. Mark side edges of
front and back 7" (7 ½", 7 ½", 8") from shoulder
seams. Matching center of sleeve to shoulder seam,
sew top edge of sleeve to sweater between side armhole markers. Sew sleeve and underarm seams.

Turtleneck: Starting at one shoulder seam, with
right side of work facing you and using circular needle, pick up 64 (68, 68, 72) stitches around neck
edge, including stitches from holders. Join stitches
and work in rounds of Knit 1, Purl 1 rib for 4".
Bind off loosely in ribbing.

*(Above) All three sweaters are
made with Colinette Point 5
wool. Here it's in a pink
and purple tweed.*

*(Opposite) Beautiful pink and
purple yarn inspired the
sweater Birdie (front left) is
wearing. The sweaters Brooke
and I are wearing are variations of the Pink and Purple
Wide Rib turtleneck.*

Project 3

PALOMINO TURTLENECK

This sweater is quite wonderful. I call it my "Palomino." I just love the tweed. I love the softness. It looks just like a Palomino horse. When I found this yarn, I just wanted to touch it. I wanted to work with it. It said: "Rub me. Squeeze me. Wear me." It spoke to me. I didn't bring anything into the knit shop that would match it, so I didn't know what I was going to wear with it. The yarn just screamed out and so I answered the call.

(Above) If you like a fat yarn, this tan and white tweed is a good choice.

(Opposite) On days when I want to feel especially nurtured, this is the sweater I reach for.

Garment Sizes

34" (36", 38", 40") to fit snugly 34" (36", 38", 40") body measurement at bust
Width of back at underarm: 17" (18", 19", 20")
Length to shoulder: 18"
Sleeve length: 17 ½"

Materials

Needles: 1 pair size 9 (5.5 mm) needles, 1 pair size 10 ½ (6.5 mm) needles or size needed to obtain gauge, cable needle, 16"-long circular needle size 9 (5.5 mm) for turtleneck
Yarn: The original yarn used in this project was a heavyweight wool, variegated ivory and tan. This yarn was used throughout the sweater.

Cable Panel

Worked on 18 stitches.
Row 1 (right side): Purl 2, Knit 6, Purl 2, Knit 6, Purl 2
Row 2 and all wrong-side rows: Knit 2, Purl 6, Knit 2, Purl 6, Knit 2
Rows 3 and 5: Repeat Row 1
Row 7 (cable twist): Purl 2, Slip 3 stitches to cable needle and hold in back of work, Knit 3, Knit 3 from cable needle, Purl 2, Slip 3 to cable needle and hold in front of work, Knit 3, Knit 3 from cable needle, Purl 2
Row 8: Repeat Row 2
Repeat these 8 rows for cable panel.

Gauge

8 stitches per 3 inches, 4 rows per inch, on larger needles

Basic Instructions

Back: On smaller needles, cast on 45 (47, 51, 53) stitches. *Work in rib as follows:* Row 1 (right side): Purl 0 (1, 3, 4), Knit 3, * Purl 3, Knit 3; repeat from *, ending Purl 0 (1, 3, 4). Row 2: Knit 0 (1, 3, 4), Purl 3, * Knit 3, Purl 3; repeat from *, ending Knit 0 (1, 3, 4). Work in rib as established for 3". Change to larger needles and work in Stockinette stitch until piece measures 6" in length. Increase 1 stitch at each edge on next row. Work even on 47 (49, 53, 55) stitches until piece measures 19" in length. Bind off 13 (13, 15, 15) stitches at beginning of next 2 rows. Slip remaining 21 (23, 23, 25) stitches onto stitch holder for back neck.

Front: Work same as back to last row of ribbing.
Next row (wrong side): Rib as established on next

15 (16, 18, 19) stitches, increase 3 stitches evenly spaced on next 15 stitches, rib to end as established 48 (50, 54, 56) stitches. *Change to larger needles and work as follows:* Next row (right side): Knit 15 (16, 18, 19), place marker on needle, work cable panel on next 18 stitches, place another marker on needle, Knit last 15 (16, 18, 19). Work cable pattern between markers and remaining stitches in Stockinette stitch. Work until piece measures 6" in length. Increase 1 stitch at each edge on next row. Work even on 50 (52, 56, 58) stitches until piece measures 16" (or 2" less than back), ending with wrong-side row.

Shape Neck: Work first 19 (20, 21, 22) stitches, drop old yarn, place center 12 (12, 14, 14) stitches on stitch holder, attach new yarn and work to end of row. Working each side of neck with its own separate yarns, bind off 3 (4, 3, 4) stitches at each neck edge once, then decrease 1 stitch at each neck edge every other row 3 times. Work even on 13 (13, 15, 15) stitches until piece measures same length as back. Bind off remaining stitches on each side loosely.

Sleeves: On smaller needles, loosely cast on 24 stitches for all sizes. Work in Knit 3, Purl 3 ribbing for 1 ¾". Change to larger needles and work in Stockinette stitch, increasing 1 stitch at each edge on next row, then every 8th row 4 times, then every 6th row 2 (3, 3, 4) times. Work even on 38 (40, 40, 42) stitches until sleeve measures 17 ½", or length desired. Bind off all stitches loosely.

Finishing: Sew shoulder seams. Mark side edges of front and back 7" (7 ½", 7 ½", 8") from shoulder seams. Matching center of sleeve to shoulder seam, sew top edge of sleeve to sweater between side armhole markers. Sew sleeve and underarm seams.

Turtleneck: Starting at one shoulder seam, with right side of work facing you and using circular needle, pick up 48 (54, 54, 54) stitches around neck edge, including stitches from holders. Join stitches and work in rounds in Knit 3, Purl 3 for 3". Bind off all stitches in ribbing.

(Left) This sweater goes so well with these corduroy riding pants that I've never worn it with anything else.

*(Clockwise from left) The thick, luscious
cable is the sweater's focal point; I wanted a clean,
uncomplicated look for this beautiful yarn; the
thicker ribbing helped give the whole piece a waist.*

95

Project 4

DENIM TURTLE WITH TWISTED BRAID TURTLENECK

This cotton turtleneck feels like a good friend to me—so comfortable, yet so unique and surprising. I was completely into turtlenecks at the time I made this, and I came across these two cotton yarns I found very appealing. There was a green with a blue fleck, and a blue with a beige fleck. Both of them felt like jeans and I could just imagine how this would fit into my daily life, where I'm in jeans nearly all the time. So I decided to use both yarns. You can see I used the light-colored yarn for the body and the sleeves, and the darker yarn for the waist ribbing, the long ribbing on the sleeves, and in stripes on the neck. I used big needles, which made the project go quickly.

(Above) To get the rustic look I wanted, I blended a ragged-edge ribbon in a gray green with a ragged-edge string in gray, green, and blue and a denim blue cotton ribbon.

(Opposite) This is one of my very favorite sweaters. It is classy and stylish, and yet goes so well with my everyday jeans.

Garment Sizes

38" (40", 42", 44") to fit loosely 34" (36", 38", 40") body measurement at bust
Width of back at underarm: 19" (20", 21", 22")
Length to shoulder: 17 ½"
Sleeve length: 18"

Materials

Needles: 1 pair size 17 (12.75 mm) needles or size needed to obtain gauge, 16"-long circular needle size 11 (8 mm) for turtleneck
Yarn: The original yarns used in this project were a dark blue braid paired with a loosely threaded filament of variegated turquoise and beige (yarn A) and a pale sea green ribbon paired with a loosely threaded filament of variegated blue and turquoise (yarn B).

Gauge

8 stitches per 3 inches, 3 rows per inch, on larger needles

Basic Instructions

Back: On straight needles, cast on 52 (52, 56, 56) stitches with yarn A. Work in Knit 2, Purl 2 rib for 2 ½", increasing 0 (2, 0, 2) stitches evenly spaced across last row 52 (54, 56,58) stitches. Cut yarn A. Attach yarn B and work in Stockinette stitch until piece measures 17 ½" in length. Bind off 15 (16, 16, 17) stitches at beginning of next 2 rows. Slip remaining 22 (22, 24, 24) stitches to a stitch holder.

Front: Work same as back until piece measures 15" (or 2 ½" less than back), ending with wrong-side row.

Adding Twisted Braid Trim

After the sweater was put together, I added the twisted braid trim. You can see the braid trim around the neck and on the mid and lower sleeves. To make twisted braid trim: Take a length of yarn about four times as long as you want the finished braid to be and fold it in half. Tie one end to a doorknob, or have a friend hold it. Then, take the other end and twist it, over and over again, until it almost starts to double up on itself. Then, fold that twisted piece in half. Hold each end, then let go. The yarn will twist itself together into trim you can add to a sweater. Make twisted braid trim with any blend of yarn colors to go with anything you can imagine.

Shape Neck: Work first 20 (21, 21, 22) stitches, drop old yarn, Slip center 12 (12, 14, 14) stitches to stitch holder. Attach new yarn B and with new yarn, work to end of row. Working each side of neck with its own separate yarns, bind off 3 stitches at each neck edge once, then decrease 1 stitch at each neck edge every other row twice. Work even on 15 (16, 16, 17) stitches until piece measures same length as back. Bind off remaining stitches on each side loosely.

Sleeves: On straight needles, loosely cast on 24 (24, 28, 28) stitches with yarn A. Work in Knit 2, Purl 2 rib for 2 ½". Continuing with yarn B, work in Stockinette stitch, increasing 1 stitch at each edge on next row, then every 4th row 8 (9, 7, 8) times and at same time, when sleeve measures 8", cut yarn A. Attach yarn B and work with yarn B for remainder of sleeve. When side increases are completed, work even on 42 (44, 44, 46) stitches until

sleeve measures 18", or length desired. Bind off all stitches loosely.

Finishing: Sew shoulder seams. Mark side edges of front and back 7 ½" (8", 8", 8 ½") from shoulder seams. Matching center of sleeve to shoulder seam, sew top edge of sleeve to sweater between side armhole markers. Sew sleeve and underarm seams.

Turtleneck: Starting at one shoulder seam, with right side of work facing you and using circular needle and yarn B, pick up 52 (52, 56, 56) stitches around neck edge, including stitches from holders. *Join stitches and work in rounds in Knit 2, Purl 2 rib as follows:* Work 3 rounds with yarn B, then 3 rounds with yarn A, 4 B, 3 A, 4 B, 1 A. With yarn A, bind off all stitches loosely in ribbing. If desired, add cord trim (see "Adding Twisted Braid Trim") to base of turtleneck, just above sleeve cuffs, and at color change on sleeves as shown.

(Left) I made this sweater specifically to go with jeans. The darker waist adds interest without bulk.

(Clockwise from left) The neckline was a perfect place to repeat the braid detail; however, I didn't want a braid at the waist, as I felt that would "bulk up" the sweater—it's really all about the sleeves; braids were sewn onto the sleeves after the piece was finished.

Project 5

RED TWEED WITH CONTRASTING NECK AND AQUA SILVER TURTLENECKS

These are dress-up, party sweaters made for weekends and holidays, or for going to the movies, the theater, or to gatherings. They're simply another variation on my basic turtleneck, but so much more dressy. I always feel pretty when I wear these two sweaters, one a red tweed with a contrasting neck, the other one an aqua silvery yarn. For each, I mixed a nubby yarn with a mohair. The nubs have some flecks of color that make it festive, and the mohair makes it so soft and luminous, almost ethereal.

(Above) For this luscious sweater, I blended a red boucle with a red mohair and a novelty multicolor.

(Opposite) You know how sometimes you see some of the same people at different parties? Well, that's why you need a couple of these sweaters in different colors.

Garment Sizes
36" (38", 40", 42") to fit 34" (36", 38", 40") body measurement at bust
Width of back at underarm: 18" (19", 20", 21")
Length to shoulder: 18"
Sleeve length: 18"

Materials
Needles: 1 pair size 17 (12.75 mm) needles or size needed to obtain gauge, 16"-long circular needle size 11 (8 mm)
Yarn: The original yarns used in this project were a medium-weight red boucle yarn blended with a red mohair and a multicolored nubby yarn with silky texture (yarn A), a medium-weight fuzzy (mohair-type) yarn (yarn B), and a single strand of the multi-colored nubby yarn with silky texture (same yarn used as part of yarn A, called yarn C when used alone). Yarn A is used for the body and sleeves; yarns B and C are used for the neck.
Notions: 2 shoulder pads

Gauge
2.5 stitches per inch, 3.5 rows per inch, on straight needles

Basic Directions
Back: On straight needles, cast on 48 (48, 52, 52) stitches with yarn A. Work in Knit 2, Purl 2 rib for 3 ½", increasing 0 (2, 0, 2) stitches evenly spaced across last row 48 (50, 52, 54) stitches. Work in Stockinette stitch until piece measures 18" in length. Bind off all stitches loosely.

Front: Work same as back until piece measures 15 ½" (or 2 ½" less than back), ending with wrong-side row.

Shape Neck: Work first 17 (18, 18, 19) stitches, drop old yarn, attach another A and with new yarn, bind off center 14 (14, 16, 16) stitches, work to end of row. Working each side of neck with its own separate yarn, bind off 2 stitches at each neck edge once, then decrease 1 stitch at each neck edge every

other row twice. Work even on 13 (14, 14, 15) stitches until piece measures same length as back. Bind off remaining stitches on each side loosely.

Sleeves: On straight needles, loosely cast on 22 (22, 26, 26) stitches with yarn A. *Row 1 (right side):* Knit 2, work in Purl 2, Knit 2 rib to end. Continue in Knit 2, Purl 2 rib as established for 3", increasing 2 (4, 0, 2) stitches on last row 24 (26, 26, 28) stitches. Work in Stockinette stitch, increasing 1 stitch at each edge every 4th row 4 times, then every 6th row 4 times. Work even on 40 (42, 42, 44) stitches until sleeve measures 18", or length desired. Bind off all stitches loosely.

Finishing: Sew shoulder seams. Mark side edges of front and back 8" (8 ¼", 8 ¼, 8 ½") from shoulder seams. Matching center of sleeve to shoulder seam, sew top edge of sleeve to sweater between side armhole markers. Sew sleeve and underarm seams.

Turtleneck: Starting at one shoulder seam, with right side of work facing you and using circular needle and yarn B, pick up 56 (56, 60, 60) stitches around neck edge. *Join stitches and work in rounds in Knit 2, Purl 2 as follows:* Work 7 rounds with yarn B, then attach yarn C and rib 1 round with yarns B and C together, 8 rounds with yarn B only, 1 yarn B and yarn C, 8 yarn B only, 1 yarn B and yarn C, 7 yarn B only. With yarn B, bind off all stitches in ribbing. Sew shoulder pads inside sweater along shoulder seam.

(Left) The length of this sweater makes it perfect match for dress pants.

(Clockwise from left) I used the multicolor boucle for subtle stripes in the neck; the ribbing is a standard Knit 2, Purl 2; this sweater has surface texture, color, and softness.

(Clockwise from left) This sweater demands diamonds;
I used an aqua mohair and a novelty multicolor yarn
with silver flecks; the yarn is so rich and interesting
that I didn't want anything special at the waist,
just a standard ribbing that is not distracting.

(Opposite) This sweater is the same pattern as the
Red Tweed with Contrasting Neck turtleneck.

V-Necks

We all evolve in our knitting over time. For me, it is enjoyable to try new yarns as well as new styles. For awhile, I was obsessed with turtlenecks and thick yarns. Then I went through my cardigan stage. With these sweaters, I began to discover the world of V-necks. They are certainly wonderful to wear. I like to layer my clothes, and V-necks are good for that. My joy in some of these projects came from combining yarns in new and exciting ways. One project, the Torn Fabric Vest, is made of yarn you can make right at home. I'd have to say that V-necks are my new thing, but wait a few months and I might just have another knitting passion!

V-Neck Projects:

1. Blue Cable
2. Brown and Khaki Cable
3. Rust and Black
4. Torn Fabric Vest

Project 1

BLUE CABLE V-NECK

This is one of my very favorite sweaters. The inspiration for this sweater came from two pairs of slacks, both of which were unique shades of blue, that I had a hard time coordinating with my other sweaters. I brought them into the knit shop and cruised around until I found a solution. I decided to mix a blue yarn that matched one of the pairs of slacks, and a second blue yarn that matched the other pair. This sweater goes perfectly with both pairs of slacks, without being too matchy-matchy. I decided on a cable V-neck because I realized that while I had already made a turtleneck cable, I had not tried a V-neck. So the experience was new and fun.

(Above) These two soft and feminine yarns are a linen and synthetic blend, and a cotton and cashmere blend.

(Opposite) I've found that a very white V-neck T-shirt under this sweater sets off the blue yarn beautifully.

Garment Sizes
34" (36", 38", 40") to fit 34" (36", 38", 40") body measurement at bust
Width of back at underarm: 17" (18", 19", 20")
Length to shoulder: 18"
Sleeve length: 13"

Materials
Needles: 1 pair size 10 (6 mm) needles, 1 pair size 11 (8 mm) needles or size needed to obtain gauge, cable needle
Yarn: The original yarns used in this project were a loosely twisted sportweight baby yarn in aqua (yarn A) and a sportweight shiny viscose yarn in off-white (yarn B). These two yarns are used together throughout the sweater.

Gauge
2.5 stitches per inch, 4 rows per inch, on larger needles

Cable Panel
Worked on 12 stitches.
Row 1 (right side): Purl 2, Knit 8, Purl 2
Row 2 and all wrong-side rows: Knit 2, Purl 8, Knit 2
Row 3: Repeat Row 1
Row 5 (cable twist): Purl 2, Slip 4 stitches to cable needle and hold in back of work, Knit 4, Knit 4 from cable needle, Purl 2
Row 7: Repeat Row 1
Row 8: Repeat Row 2
Repeat these 8 rows for cable panel.

Basic Instructions
Back: On smaller needles, cast on 46 (48, 50, 52) stitches with yarns A and B. Work in Knit 1, Purl 1 rib for 1". Change to larger needles, Knit across, decreasing 1 stitch at each end of row. Starting with Purl row on wrong side, work in Stockinette stitch, decreasing 1 stitch at each edge every 4th row

3 times more. Work even on 38 (40, 42, 44) stitches until piece measures 6" in length. Then increase 1 stitch at each edge every 4th row 3 times. Work even on 44 (46, 48, 50) stitches until piece measures 11" (10 ¾", 10 ¼", 10") in length, ending with wrong-side row.

Shape Armholes: Bind off 2 stitches at beginning of next 2 rows. Decrease 1 stitch at each armhole edge every other row twice. Work even on 36 (38, 40, 42) stitches until piece measures 18" in length. Bind off all stitches loosely.

Front: On smaller needles, cast on 44 (46, 48, 50) stitches with yarns A and B. Work in Knit 1, Purl 1 rib for 1". *Change to larger needles and work as follows:* Next row (right side): Knit 3, increase 1 stitch in next stitch, Knit 13 (14, 15, 16), place marker on needle, Purl 2, Knit 1, increase as before, Knit 1, increase, Knit 2, Purl 2, place another marker on needle, Knit 12 (13, 14, 15), increase, Knit 4 48 (50, 52, 54) stitches. (*Note:* There is no waistline shaping on front at side edges as there was on back.) *Following row (wrong side):* Starting with Row 2 of cable panel, work cable panel between markers and work remaining stitches in Stockinette stitch, starting with Purl row. Work same as back until piece measures 10 ½" (10 ½", 10 ¼", 10"), ending with wrong-side row.

Shape V-Neck and Armholes: Work V-neck when piece measures 10 ½" and at same time, shape armholes when piece measures 11" (10 ¾", 10 ¼", 10"). (On two smaller sizes, begin V-neck shaping first; on two larger sizes, begin armhole shaping first.) *To shape armholes:* Bind off 3 stitches at beginning of next 2 rows. At each armhole edge, decrease 1 stitch every other row twice. *To shape V-neck:* On right-side row, work to last 3 Knit stitches before cable panel, Knit 2 Together (left front neck decrease), Knit 1, Slip marker, Purl 2, Knit first 4 cable stitches, drop yarns, attach new yarns A and B and with new yarns, Knit remaining 4 stitches of cable, Purl 2, Slip marker, Knit 1, Slip 1 stitch, Knit 1, Pass Slip Stitch Over (right front neck decrease), work to end. Continue working each side with its own separate yarn, decreasing 1 stitch at each neck edge every other row 6 (7, 7, 8) times more and complete armhole shaping. Work on remaining 12 (12, 13, 13) stitches on each side until piece measures same length as back. Bind off remaining stitches on each side loosely.

Sleeves: On smaller needles, loosely cast on 24 (26, 26, 28) stitches with yarns A and B. Work in Knit 1, Purl 1 rib for 1 ¼". Change to larger needles and work in Stockinette stitch, increasing 1 stitch at each edge every 8th row 4 times. Work even on 32 (34, 34, 36) stitches until sleeve measures 13", or length desired.

Shape Cap: Bind off 2 stitches at beginning of next 2 rows. Decrease 1 stitch at each edge on every other row until cap measures 4". Bind off all remaining stitches loosely.

Finishing: Leaving center 14 (16, 16, 18) bound-off stitches unworked for back neckline, sew shoulder seams, easing remaining stitches of back to fit front shoulder stitches. Sew underarm seams. Sew sleeve seams. Matching center top of sleeve to shoulder seam, sew sleeve cap to shaped armhole.

(Left) The short ribbing on the sleeve allows just enough flexibility to push the sleeves up if I like.

*(Clockwise from left) The neck of this sweater is
curvy and sensuous; I wanted the sleeves to fit
snugly, so the sweater would look nice under suits;
the narrow ribbing at the waist makes a delicate detail.*

Project 2

BROWN AND KHAKI CABLE V-NECK

As soon as I finished my blue cable V-neck, I started thinking about the rolled neck and how it continues down, twisting itself into the cable. I thought it might be fun to have contrasting colors twisted in the cable and then continue up on either side for a contrasting neck roll. I chose a ribbon yarn, the same type I had tried for the first time on my Long Red Ribbon cardigan, but it was more substantial. I found a really colorful ribbon with oranges, browns, and blues. Then, I mixed it with a khaki ribbon for one side of the sweater, and then mixed it with a brown ribbon for the other side.

(Above) Three nylon ribbons make up this sweater: brown, khaki, and a multicolor.

(Opposite) Even though the two sides of this sweater are based on contrasting colors there is a colorful ribbon common to both sides that softens the contrast.

Garment Sizes

30" (34", 38") to fit snugly 32" (36", 40") body measurement at bust (*Note:* This garment is quite narrow when lying flat, but stretches sideways when worn. You may wish to knit the pieces a bit longer to accommodate the stretching, or simply knit a larger size.)
Width of back at underarm: 15" (17", 19")
Length to shoulder: 17"
Sleeve length: 12"

Materials

Needles: 1 pair size 10 (6 mm) needles, 1 pair size 11 (8 mm) needles or size needed to obtain gauge, cable needle
Yarn: The original yarns used in this project were ⅛"-wide variegated multicolored ribbon (yarn A), and ⅜"-wide ribbon in beige (yarn B) and in brown (yarn C). Yarns A and B are worked together for the back, left front, and left sleeve. Yarns A and C are worked together for the right front and right sleeve.

Gauge

3.3 stitches per inch, 4 rows per inch, on larger needles

Cable Panel

Worked on 12 stitches.
Row 1 (right side): Purl 2, Knit 8, Purl 2
Row 2 and all wrong-side rows: Knit 2, Purl 8, Knit 2
Row 3: Repeat Row 1
Row 5 (cable twist): Purl 2, Slip 4 stitches to cable needle and hold in back of work, Knit 4, Knit 4 from cable needle, Purl 2
Row 7: Repeat Row 1
Row 8: Repeat Row 2
Repeat these 8 rows for cable panel.

Basic Instructions

Back: On smaller needles, cast on 50 (56, 64) stitches with yarns A and B. Work in Knit 1, Purl 1 rib for 1 ¼". Change to larger needles, Knit across,

Go Collarless

A lot of people love to
knit, but dislike putting
sweaters together.
I'm in that category,
so I pay the knit shop
to finish my sweaters.
If paying a knit shop
to finish your sweaters
is not an option, look
for patterns that call
for minimal finishing.
For instance, this
sweater has no collar,
as the rolled collar
is knit right into the
garment. With this pat-
tern, adding a collar is
one finishing task you
don't have to tackle.

decreasing 1 stitch at each end of row. Starting with Purl row on wrong side, work in Stockinette stitch, decreasing 1 stitch at each edge every 4th row twice more. Work even on 44 (50, 58) stitches until piece measures 5 ½" in length. Then increase 1 stitch at each edge every 4th row 3 times. Work even on 50 (56, 64) stitches until piece measures 10" (9 ¾", 9 ½") in length, ending with wrong-side row.

Shape Armholes: Bind off 3 stitches at beginning of next 2 rows. Decrease 1 stitch at each armhole edge every other row twice. Work even on 40 (46, 54) stitches until piece measures 17" in length. Bind off all stitches loosely.

Front: On smaller needles, cast on 25 (28, 32) stitches with yarns A and C, drop yarns A and C; attach ball of A and B and with new yarns, cast on 25 (28, 32) more stitches. Work each half-row with its own separate yarn, always twisting yarns on wrong side when you change colors (bringing new color up from under old color), working 50 (56, 64) stitches in Knit 1, Purl 1 rib for 1 ¼". *Change to larger needles and work as follows:* Next row (right side): Knit 1, increase 1 stitch in next stitch, Knit 18 (21, 25), place marker on needle, Purl 2, Knit 1, increase as before, Knit 1, change colors, increase, Knit 2, Purl 2, place another marker on needle, Knit 17 (20, 24), increase, Knit 2 54 (60, 68) stitches. (*Note:* There is no waistline shaping on front at side edges as there was on back.) *Following row (wrong side):* Starting with Row 2 of cable panel, work cable panel between markers and work remaining stitches in Stockinette stitch, starting with Purl row. As you twist cable, continue to work each half of cable in its original color. Work same as back until piece measures 10" (9 ¾", 9 ½"), ending with wrong-side row.

Shape V-Neck and Armholes: Work V-neck when piece measures about 10" and 5th cable twist is completed and at same time, shape armholes when piece measures 10" (9 ¾", 9 ½"). On smaller size, begin V-neck and armhole shaping on same row; on two larger sizes, begin armhole shaping first. *To shape armholes:* Bind off 3 stitches at beginning of next 2 rows. At each armhole edge, decrease 1 stitch every other row twice. *To shape V-neck:* (*Note:* After work is divided, maintain original color of 4 cable stitches that continue up V-neck edge on each side.) On right-side row, work to last 3 Knit stitches before cable panel, Knit 2 Together (left front neck decrease), Knit 1, Slip marker, Purl 2, Knit first 4 cable stitches, drop yarns, attach new yarns and with new yarns, Knit remaining 4 stitches of cable, Purl 2, Slip marker, Knit 1, Slip 1 stitch, Knit 1, Pass Slip Stitch Over (right front neck decrease), work to end. Continue working each side with its own separate yarn, decreasing 1 stitch at each neck edge every other row 7 (8, 9) times more and complete armhole shaping. Work on remaining 14 (16, 19) stitches on each side until piece measures same length as back. Bind off remaining stitches on each side loosely.

Left Sleeve: On smaller needles, loosely cast on 26 (28, 30) stitches with yarns A and B. Work in Knit 1, Purl 1 rib for 1 ¼". Change to larger needles and work in Stockinette stitch, increasing 1 stitch at each edge on next row, then every 3" 3 times. Work even on 34 (36, 38) stitches until sleeve measures 12", or length desired.

Shape Cap: Bind off 2 stitches at beginning of next 2 rows. Decrease 1 stitch at each edge on every other row until cap measures 3 ½". Bind off 2 stitches at beginning of next 4 rows. Bind off all remaining stitches loosely.

Right Sleeve: With yarns A and C, work to correspond to first sleeve.

Finishing: Leaving center 14 (16, 18) bound-off stitches unworked for back neckline, sew shoulder seams, easing remaining stitches of back to fit front shoulder stitches. Sew underarm seams. Sew sleeve seams. Matching center top of sleeve to shoulder seam, sew sleeve cap to shaped armhole on each side.

(Clockwise from left) Each side is its own color, right down to the hem. With the two alternating colors, you can see better how cables are engineered; I wanted this summer sweater to fit snuggly, yet be able to be worn with a shirt underneath; I kept the sleeves simple—I didn't want anything to take away from the drama going down the front.

Project 3

RUST AND BLACK V-NECK

This is another sweater inspired by a pair of shoes that didn't go with anything. I love these shoes, but they're an odd rust color with black trim. I'd had these shoes five years, but rarely wore them. So I took them to the yarn shop and I found this cotton yarn that was striped with the same exact color as my shoes. Ordinarily I wouldn't knit with just one strand, not since discovering how much fun it is to blend yarns. I have to admit this was pretty boring to knit, row after row after row. But then came the fun part: embellishing it with black antique buttons sewn on with contrasting thread. It has become a wonderful sweater for me.

(Above) This is a cotton ribbon shoelace yarn in black and rust.

(Opposite) I took my shoes to the knit shop to find a yarn that matched. That was much easier than trying to find a ready-made sweater to match.

Garment Sizes

34" (36", 38", 40") to fit snugly 34" (36", 38", 40") body measurement at bust
Width of back at underarm: 17" (18", 19", 20")
Length to shoulder: 18 ½"
Sleeve length: 11"

Materials

Needles: 1 pair size 10 (6 mm) needles, 1 pair size 10 ½ (6.5 mm) needles or size needed to obtain gauge, crochet hook size J (6 mm) for trim
Yarn: The original yarn used in this project was a soft woven ribbon with black and orange bands. This yarn is used throughout the sweater.
Notions: 9 small buttons for decoration

Gauge

3.75 stitches per inch, 6 rows per inch, on larger needles

Basic Instructions

Back: On smaller needles, cast on 64 (68, 72, 76) stitches. Work in Knit 2, Purl 2 rib for 1 ½". Change to larger needles and work in Stockinette stitch until piece measures 11" (11", 10 ¾", 10 ¾"), ending with wrong-side row.

Shape Armholes: *Next row (right side):* Knit 1, Knit 2 Together (decrease), Knit to last 3 stitches, Slip 1, Knit 1, Pass Slip Stitch Over (decrease), Knit 1. Purl 1 row. Repeat these 2 rows 7 (7, 8, 8) times more. Work even on 48 (52, 54, 58) stitches until piece measures 18 ½" in length. Bind off all stitches loosely.

Front: Work same as back until piece measures same as back to armhole shaping, ending with wrong-side row.

Shape Armholes and V-Neck: Shape armholes as for back and at same time, when piece measure 13",

CONSIDER THIS

Using Old Buttons

I got the black buttons on this sweater from an antique dress, like you'd find at a flea market or thrift store. If you see an old dress that costs just a few dollars, even if it's not your size, style, or it's stained or damaged, but it has really great old buttons, buy it and keep the buttons for something special.

shape V-neck as follows: *Next right-side row:* Work to last 3 stitches before center front, Slip 1, Knit 1, Pass Slip Stitch Over, Knit 1, drop old yarn, attach new yarn and with new yarn, Knit 1, Knit 2 Together, work to end. Working each side with its own separate yarn, work neck decreases every other row 11 (11, 12, 12) times more. Work even on 12 (14, 14, 16) stitches until piece measures same length as back. Bind off remaining stitches on each side loosely.

Sleeves: On smaller needles, loosely cast on 40 (40, 44, 44) stitches. Work in Knit 2, Purl 2 rib for 1 ½". Change to larger needles and work in Stockinette stitch, increasing 1 stitch at each edge on next row then every 6th row 4 (5, 4, 5) times. Work even on 50 (52, 54, 56) stitches until sleeve measures 11", or length desired to underarm.

Shape Cap: Bind off 2 stitches at beginning of every row until cap measures 3", then bind off 4 (5, 5, 6) stitches at beginning of next 2 rows. Bind off all remaining stitches loosely.

Finishing: Sew shoulder and underarm seams. Sew sleeve seams. Matching center top of sleeve to shoulder seam, sew sleeve caps to shaped armhole on each side. Crochet single row around neck, spacing stitches to keep edge flat and smooth. Sew on decorative buttons, one at center and four spaced evenly up each side of V-neck as shown.

(Left) I love these shoes but couldn't find anything to wear with them. So I hit my local yarn shop and found a skein that matches perfectly.

(Clockwise from left) I usually mix yarns to get the colors
I want, but this yarn was already striped with the rust and
black I needed; I purposely used different thread patterns
to sew on the buttons; the yarn is so rich and interesting
that I didn't feel I wanted anything special at the waist,
just a standard ribbing that is not distracting.

119

Project 4

TORN FABRIC VEST

I bought the yarn for this vest in New York City. I had never seen anything like it in my life and it was expensive. I didn't want to buy a lot, so I decided to make a vest. It's a very simple vest, but made from this yarn, it looks quite interesting—a real attention-getter. This yarn is basically made of strips of torn fabric tied together with eyelash yarn. That's it. After I started thinking about it, I realized I could make this yarn myself. So I got some cotton fabric and tore it into ¼"- to ½"-wide strips, tied them together in a long string with eyelash yarn, and twisted the string into a very inexpensive ball of yarn.

(Above) This is a very expensive torn fabric yarn (which I later copied for pennies) and a colorful yarn, trimmed with a shiny Anny Blatt yarn called Victoria.

(Opposite) My daughter, Birdie, models this off-beat vest. I had such a good time designing it.

Garment Sizes

36" (38", 40", 42") to fit 34" (36", 38", 40") body measurement at bust
Width of back at underarm: 18" (19", 20", 21")
Length to shoulder: 23"

Materials

Needles: 1 pair size 10 (6 mm) needles, 1 pair size 10 ½ (6.5 mm) needles or size needed to obtain gauge, crochet hook size J (6 mm) for trim
Yarn: The original yarn used in this project came from assorted cotton fabrics cut into ½"-wide strips, knotted end to end with 1" ends left untrimmed to form "flags" and paired with a strand of eyelash yarn (yarn A) and a soft, shiny woven cord (yarn B). Yarn A was used for knitting the vest; yarn B was used for the crocheted border trim.
Notions: 5 buttons

Gauge

2.9 stitches per inch on larger needles

Basic Instructions

Back: On smaller needles, cast on 52 (55, 58, 60) stitches with yarn A. Work in Garter stitch (Knit every row) for 4 rows. Change to larger needles and work in Stockinette stitch until piece measures 12" in length for all sizes, ending with wrong-side row.

Shape Armholes: Bind off 2 stitches at beginning of next 4 rows. Decrease 1 stitch at each armhole edge every other row 3 times. Work even on 38 (41, 44, 46) stitches until piece measures 23" in length. Bind off all stitches loosely.

Left Front: On smaller needles, cast on 26 (27, 29, 30) stitches. Work in Garter stitch for 4 rows. Change to larger needles and work in Stockinette stitch until piece measures 8 ½", ending with wrong-side row.

Shape V-Neck and Armhole: Work to last 2 stitches, Knit 2 Together (neck decrease). Work neck decrease

Making Torn Fabric Yarn

Another way to make your own torn fabric yarn is to search a thrift store for flannel nightgowns and pajamas you won't mind ripping up. Flannel makes perfect torn fabric strips, and it knits into a very holiday-looking scarf. You want to use very big needles for this. I made my daughter a torn fabric scarf and she loves it.

every 4th row 7 (7, 8, 8) times more and at same time, when piece measures same as back to armhole shaping, shape armhole as follows: At arm edge bind off 2 stitches at beginning of each next 2 right-side rows, then decrease 1 stitch at armhole edge every other row 3 times. When decreases at armhole and neck edges are completed, work even on 11 (12, 13, 14) stitches until piece measures same length as back. Bind off all remaining stitches.

Right Front: Work to correspond to Left Front, reversing all shaping.

Finishing: Sew shoulder and underarm seams.

Crocheted Trim: With right side of work facing you, starting on one armhole at underarm seam with crochet hook and yarn B, crochet row of single crochet all around armhole edge, spacing stitches to keep edge flat and smooth. Join to first single crochet, then work row of reverse single crochet (working left to right) around armhole. Join to first stitch and fasten off. Repeat on other armhole edge. Turn jacket upside down with right side of work facing you. Starting at lower edge at left underarm seam, crochet row of single crochet all around jacket edge, working across bottom, up right front, around neck, down left front, and back across bottom to starting point; do not cut yarn. On left front, determine placement of 5 buttons along left front edge with top button at start of V-neck, lowest button at bottom and others spaced evenly between. With safety pins, mark corresponding placement for buttonholes on right front. Now work row of reverse single crochet around jacket edge, working buttonhole at each safety pin marker as follows: Chain 1, Skip 1 single crochet, work in next single crochet. Fasten off when row is completed. Sew buttons to left front opposite buttonholes.

(Left) The fabric this yarn creates is crazy, mixed up, and one of a kind. Crocheted edging outlines this vest.

(Clockwise from left) The ribbon trim is on the arm openings as well as the front opening; the hem features the same black ribbon trim; the buttons were chosen to be fun.

Fun & Fast

Throughout this book, I have focused mostly on sweaters. That is what I'm known for, and that is what I love doing. But if you're new to knitting, or returning to the craft, you might find sweaters daunting. It's best to start out with simpler projects, such as a scarf, shawl, or satchel. With the help of a friend who knits, a great aunt, or a companion basic knitting book, you can learn the four main knitting functions—cast on, bind off, knit, and purl—and then put those new skills to work with the projects in this chapter. Later on, when you learn to increase, decrease—which is how you shape sleeves, armholes, and necks—you're ready to try most of the sweaters in this book.

Extra Projects:

1. **Evening Shawl**
2. **Chunky Scarf**
3. **String Satchel**
4. **Torn Flannel Placemat**
5. **Green Lurex Shell**
6. **Multi-Chunk Boatneck Shell**

Project 1

EVENING SHAWL

I made this shawl for my daughter, Brooke. She wanted something light and festive and I was in the mood to create something as beautiful and exciting as she is. I chose a shocking pink mohair and mixed it with a pink ribbon yarn with gold threads. The mohair gives it warmth and the ribbon gives it sass. After it was done, I added a fringe using the ribbon only, and then I added beads to the fringe, both to add interest and to give the fringe some weight to help it lie flat.

CONSIDER THIS

Dressing up Fringe

When I add fringe, I want it to look juicy and wonderful. To me, nothing looks worse than skinny fringe. So I don't suggest skimping here; I suggest extravagance. Consider adding interest (and using up some leftover yarn) by incorporating other colors of yarn in the fringe, even if that yarn is not in the shawl.

Shawl Measurements

About 20" wide x 60" long, or length desired. (*Note:* Shawl stretches easily to wrap as a wider or longer shawl as desired.)

Materials

Needles: 1 pair size 15 (10 mm) needles or size needed to obtain gauge, crochet hook size K (6.5 mm) for fringe

Yarn: The original yarn used in this project was a ⅜"-wide woven ribbon paired with a thin strand of mohair, both in bright pink.

Notions: About 150 gold beads, about 6 mm in diameter, with hole large enough to thread ribbon through, and long-eyed tapestry or beading needle.

Gauge

2 stitches per inch

Basic Instructions

Cast on 40 stitches with ribbon and mohair held together. Work in Garter stitch (Knit every row) for 60" or length desired. Bind off all stitches.

Fringe: Cut 5 16" lengths of ribbon for each fringe (there are 16 fringes on each end). Hold five ribbon lengths together and fold in half. With crochet hook draw folded end through edge of shawl to form small loop. Draw ends of ribbon through loop, then gently pull on ends to tighten fringe. Place about 16 fringes along each end of shawl. Thread a bead onto 4 to 6 separate strands of each fringe, threading ribbon into needle to draw it through bead more easily. Knot ribbon just below bead to hold in place. Position beads at various heights along fringe.

(Far left) This is an elegant hot pink ribbon made by Katia, mixed with a mohair and trimmed with beads.

(Right) My daughter, Brooke, wore this shawl for New Year's Eve. I loved making it, and Brooke loved wearing it.

Project 2

CHUNKY SCARF

I made this scarf to go with my beige Random Purl turtleneck. Both are made with very thick wool yarn, and I wear them together when I want to be very, very warm. My finished scarf measures 10" wide x 72" (64" without fringe) long, but you can make it any length or width you like.

CONSIDER THIS

Creating Your Own Pattern

To get this stitch pattern, I played around and experimented. I tried this and that and undid what I didn't like. Finally I hit on a pattern of stitches that felt right. I had so much fun playing around like that. Try out different knits and purls on a scarf until it rings your chimes. Instead of following my stitches precisely, try some variations and see how they feel to you.

Scarf Measurements
About 10" wide x 64" long, or length desired, plus 8" fringe added at each end

Materials
Needles: 1 pair size 15 (10 mm) needles or size needed to obtain gauge, crochet hook size K (10 mm) for fringe
Yarn: The original yarn used in this project was a heavyweight thick and thin wool yarn in off-white.

Gauge
2.6 stitches per inch

Pattern Stitch
Multiple of 5 stitches, plus 1.
Row 1: Knit 1, * Purl 4, Knit 1; repeat from * across
Row 2: Purl 1, * Knit 4, Purl 1; repeat from * across
Rows 3 through 6: Repeat Rows 1 and 2 twice more

Row 7: Knit across
Row 8: Purl 2, * Knit 3, Purl 2; repeat from * across, ending Knit 2, Purl 2
Row 9: Knit 2, Purl 2, * Knit 2, Purl 3; repeat from * across, ending Knit 2
Rows 10 through 13: Repeat Rows 8 and 9 twice more
Row 14: Knit across
Repeat these 14 rows for pattern.

Basic Instructions
Scarf: Cast on 26 stitches. Work in pattern stitch for desired length. Bind off.

Fringe: Cut 6 17" lengths for each fringe. (There are 5 fringes on each end.) Hold 6 yarn lengths together and fold in half. With crochet hook, draw folded end through edge of scarf to form small loop. Draw yarn ends through loop, then gently pull on ends to tighten fringe.

(Left) The Chunky Scarf is my own unique combination of stitches. Friends ask me, "Where did you get that scarf?" I'm proud of the things I make.

(Far left) This is the same Muench Marokko I used for my beige Random Purl turtleneck.

(Right) My daughter, Birdie, shows off my Chunky Scarf, which I enjoy getting out of my closet every winter.

Project 3

STRING SATCHEL

I wanted to knit a book bag for my daughter, Birdie, who is in high school. Knitting is big with kids, and you see them knitting everywhere—on the bus, in the park, at coffee houses, at after-school knitting clubs. But if you're knitting something for a teenager, it must have the "cool" factor. I thought a book bag made of sturdy jute twine would be just that. Birdie loves it!

(Above) This is common jute used in an uncommon manner.

(Opposite) When your kids are babies, you can knit just about anything and they won't object to wearing it. But when they get into school, they tend to be more particular. My teenage daughter, Birdie, found this bag much to her liking.

Satchel Measurements
About 16" wide x 12" deep

Materials
Needles: 1 pair size 15 (10 mm) needles or size needed to obtain gauge, yarn needle with large eye
Yarn: The original yarn used in this project was a double strand of medium duty jute twine, about 200 yards.

Gauge
2 stitches per inch

Basic Instructions
Cast on 30 stitches using 2 strands of twine. Work in Garter stitch (Knit every row) for 32 rows. Bind off.

Finishing: Lay piece flat, then fold bottom 12" end up to within 3" of top edge to make pocket. Sew side edges of pocket together with twine, and turn pocket inside out with seam enclosed.

Braided strap: Determine length of strap desired and cut twine long enough to make braided strap of desired length, cutting 8 strands of twine for each of the 3 braid sections. Secure twine strands together at 1 end and braid 3 thick sections together neatly to make strap in length desired. Secure end of finished braid by sewing across strands. With single strand of twine, sew strap ends securely to bag at each side edge of pocket.

CONSIDER THIS
Knitting Just About Anything

At left you see another satchel I knit, this time out of strips torn from a pair of Levis I got from my co-author, Kathy. When most people think of knitting, they think of wool yarn. But knitting refers to the stitch, not the material. You can use anything you want, from string, ribbon, and torn fabric, to wool and cotton cording.

Project 4

TORN FLANNEL PLACEMAT

I had some handmade yarn leftover after I made a couple of scarves for my daughters. I loved the yarn so much that I started casting about for another project. My eyes came to rest on my lively red, blue, and yellow dishes, which are visible in my kitchen since I've taken off the cabinet doors. I thought the reds in the flannel would work perfectly with the primary colors of my dishes.

(Above) Here's my handmade torn fabric yarn, this time used without eyelash yarn for the placemat.

(Opposite) Can you believe this placemat is made from a knit created from a cut-up flannel nightgown?

Placemat Measurements
About 12" x 18"

Materials
Needles: 1 pair size 17 (12.75 mm) needles or size needed to obtain gauge
Yarn: Torn flannel strips, ¼" to ½" wide, tied end to end

Gauge
2.5 stitches per inch

Basic Instructions
Cast on 36 stitches. Work in Garter stitch (Knit every row) until piece measures 18". Bind off all stitches.

CONSIDER THIS
Choosing Trim Colors

I left the edges plain on my placemat, but you could crochet a trim around the outer edge if you wanted. A trim color helps play up whichever color you want in a multicolored fabric.

Black trim would add a certain sophistication, while a dark green trim would work well in a dining room with a lot of greens. A vibrant red would introduce a punch of color,

perfect for a kitchen. I'm in love with an Anny Blatt shiny ribbon called Victoria. That's what I used for trim on my Torn Fabric Vest and it feels so good to the touch.

Project 5

GREEN LUREX SHELL

I loved knitting this shell. It went very fast, and I didn't have to send it to
a finisher (which is what I normally do with my sweaters) because it is knit
in the round—no side seams, and no sleeves. All that's left are the shoulder
seams, and that I can do. It was done and on my back in a week. This lively
shell solved a need I had for something light to wear with a denim suit.
I wanted a hand-knit look, but I didn't want anything too bulky. I loved
the idea of doing a ribbing on both the bottom and the top, which I thought
added a bit of interest. This is one of those pieces that turned out to fit better
than I expected.

*(Above) Here is that same
Colinette Point 5, this time
in a multicolor, I used in
many other sweaters.*

*(Opposite) I used three colors
of the same viscose and lurex
yarn for the Green Lurex
Shell: a green, a black,
and an off-white.*

Garment Sizes
33" (36 ½", 40") to fit snugly 33" (36", 39")
body measurement at bust
Width of back at underarm: 16 ¾" (18 ¼", 20")
Length to shoulder: 17"

Materials
Needles: 1 pair size 9 (5.5 mm) needles or size
needed to obtain gauge
Yarn: The original yarns used in this project were
a sportweight yarn in green with green sparkle
filament (yarn A), in white with silver sparkle
filament (yarn B), and in black with black sparkle
filament (yarn C). Yarn A was used as the main
color, and yarns B and C were used for the
geometric design bands.

Gauge:
5 stitches per inch, 7 rows per inch

Checkerboard Pattern
Worked on multiple of 4 stitches with yarns B
and C.
Row 1 (right side): * Knit 2 C, Knit 2 B; repeat
from * across
Row 2: * Purl 2 B, Purl 2 C; repeat from * across
Row 3: * Knit 2 B, Knit 2 C; repeat from * across
Row 4: * Purl 2 C, Purl 2 B; repeat from * across
Rows 5 and 6: Repeat Rows 1 and 2 once more

Basic Instructions
Back: Cast on 84 (92, 100) stitches with yarn A.
Work rib as follows: Row 1 (right side): Knit 4,
work in Purl 4, Knit 4 rib to end. *Following row:*
Purl 4, work in Knit 4, Purl 4 rib to end. Repeat
these 2 rows until ribbing is 1 ½". *Now work
geometric design bands as follows:* Work Rows 1
through 6 of checkerboard pattern. Continuing in
Stockinette stitch, work 1 row with A, 2 rows B,
1 row C, 2 rows B, 2 rows A. Work Rows 1 through

4 of checkerboard pattern twice. Work 1 row with B, 2 rows C, 1 row A, 1 row C, 1 row B, 1 row C, 2 rows A. Work Rows 1 through 6 of checkerboard pattern once. Now work with yarn A only for remainder of back. Work even until piece measures 11 ½" (11", 10 ½"), ending with wrong-side row.

Shape Armholes: *Next row (right side):* Knit 2, Purl 2, Slip 1, Knit 1, Pass Slip Stitch Over (decrease made), Knit to last 6 stitches, Knit 2 Together (another decrease), Purl 2, Knit 2. *Following row:* Purl 2, Knit 2, Purl to last 4 stitches, Knit 2, Purl 2.

Repeat these last 2 rows 5 times more 72 (80, 88) stitches. Work even in Stockinette stitch, continuing 4-stitch pattern at each armhole edge (without decreases) until piece measures 16" in length. Work in Knit 4, Purl 4 rib for 1". Bind off all stitches loosely in ribbing.

Front: Work same as for Back.

Finishing: Sew underarm seams. Starting at armhole edge, sew 1 ¾" seam at each shoulder, leaving wide opening for neck.

(Left) I made this pattern as I went along— it was not difficult.

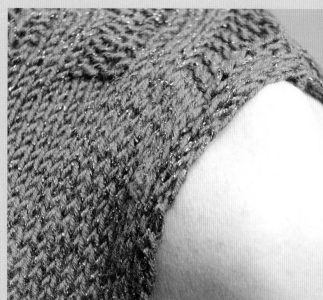

(Clockwise from left) This clean neckline works well under a suit; the arm openings are cut in, which is very flattering; notice the interesting ribbing on the waist.

Project 6

MULTI-CHUNK BOATNECK SHELL

This colorful shell is a wonderful adaptation of the previous Green Lurex Shell. I loved the way that one turned out, and I wanted another shell that I could wear with jeans during the summer. I found this wonderful multi-colored yarn and went to town. I decided to not make the design complicated—so the project went fast and I couldn't be happier with the results.

(Above) This multicolored yarn is a heavyweight wool.

Garment Sizes
32" (36", 40"), to fit snugly 32" (36", 40") body measurement at bust
Width of back at underarm: 16" (18", 20")
Length to shoulder: 19"

Materials
Needles: 24"-long circular needle Size 10 ½ (6.5 mm) needles or size needed to obtain gauge
Yarn: The original yarn used in this project was a heavyweight wool variegated in bright colors. This yarn was used throughout sweater.

Gauge
3 stitches per inch, 4 rows per inch

The Basic Directions
Sweater: With circular needle, cast on 96 (108, 120) stitches. Join stitches and work in rounds in Knit 3, Purl 3 for 2". Work in Stockinette stitch until piece measures 12" (12", 11 ½", 11 ½") in length.

Shape Armholes: Slip 48 (54, 60) stitches to a stitch holder and work back and forth on remaining 48 (54, 60) stitches as follows: *Row 1 (right side):* Purl 2, Knit 2, Purl 2, Slip 1, Knit 1, Pass Slip Stitch Over (decrease made), Knit to last 8 stitches, Knit 2 Together (decrease made), Purl 2, Knit 2, Purl 2. Following row (wrong side): Knit 2, Purl 2, Knit 2, Purl to last 6 stitches, Knit 2, Purl 2, Knit 2. Repeat these 2 rows 2 (3, 4) times more. Work even on 42 (46, 50) stitches until armhole is 5", ending with a wrong side row. *Next row:* Purl 2, work in Knit 2, Purl 2 rib to end. Continue to work in Knit 2, Purl rib as established for 2". Bind off in ribbing. Transfer remaining 48 (54, 60) stitches from holder back onto circular needle and complete to correspond to first half.

Finishing: Starting from armhole edge, sew 1 ½" shoulder seam on each side, leaving a wide opening for neck.

(Clockwise from left) My daughter, Brooke, models the Multi-Chunk Boatneck Shell, a variation of the Green Lurex Shell; the arm openings are cut in, which is very flattering; notice the interesting ribbing on the waist.

List of Yarns

I've included what I know about the yarns I used in these sweaters and projects, but I'm not expecting you to rush out and try to find these exact yarns. Yarn companies are continually updating their lines, eliminating some types and colors, and adding others. Yarns come in and out of fashion, like fabrics and styles. So what's available now might not be available next month. On the other hand, yarns that do not exist now might be introduced in the future. So keep your eyes open. Truth be told, yarn selection often boils down to what's at the yarn shop, or what's on sale. So the idea is to get inspired by the yarns you find, and then combine them with other yarns to achieve the thickness, surface interest, and feel you want.

Pullovers

Basic Rust Mohair
Pages 24-27
Yarn 1 of 2:
Contents: Merino wool
Color: Rust

Yarn 2 of 2:
Contents: Mohair
Color: Rust

Pumpkin Patch
Pages 28-31
Yarn 1 of 2:
Style: Novelty boucle
Contents: Cotton
Color: Multicolor with gold thread

Yarn 2 of 2:
Contents: Mohair
Color: Olive

Taupe Angora Tweed
Pages 32-35
Yarn 1 of 2:
Contents: Wool
Color: Heather tweed

Yarn 2 of 2:
Contents: Angora
Color: Taupe

Sherbet Scoop Neck
Pages 36-39
Yarn 1 of 1:
Brand: Filatura Di Crosa
Style: Aiko
Contents: Cashmere and synthetic
Colors: Various

Reversible Boatneck
Pages 40-43
Yarn 1 of 3:
Brand: Katia
Style: Twist
Contents: Acrylic and cotton
Color: Blue multicolor

Yarn 2 of 3:
Style: Ribbon
Color: Beige

Yarn 3 of 3:
Brand: Katia
Style: Twist
Contents: Acrylic and cotton
Color: Beige

Carnival
Pages 44-47
Yarn 1 of 3:
Brand: Stacy Charles
Style: Samba
Contents: Cotton
Color: Purple multicolor

Yarn 2 of 3:
Brand: Stacy Charles
Style: Samba
Contents: Cotton
Color: Red multicolor

Yarn 3 of 3:
Brand: Noro
Style: Wakaba
Contents: Cotton
Color: Multicolor

Cardigans

Iowa Gray

Mylar Tweed
Pages 50-53
Yarn 1 of 1:
Contents: Mohair with metallic flecks
Color: Gray

Gray Chenille
Pages 54-57
Yarn 1 of 1:
Style: Chenille
Contents: Synthetic
Color: Koala gray

Black Multi-Tweed
Pages 58-61
Yarn 1 of 3:
Style: Boucle
Color: Black

Yarn 2 of 3:
Contents: Mohair
Color: Black

Yarn 3 of 3:
Style: Novelty
Color: Black flag and multicolor

Flag
Pages 62-65
Yarn 1 of 2:
Brand: Filatura Di Crosa
Style: Magia novelty flag with mohair
Contents: Mohair, polyamid, and acrylic
Color: Multicolor

Yarn 2 of 2:
Brand: Stacy Charles
Style: Twisted stripe
Contents: Wool
Color: Blue and white tweed

Colorful Tennis
Pages 66-69
Yarn 1 of 2:
Brand: Rowan
Style: Malibu boucle braid
Contents: Cotton
Color: Multicolor

Yarn 2 of 2 (trim):
Brand: Noro
Style: Cash Iroha
Contents: Cashmere and silk
Color: Midnight blue

Scotland
Pages 70-73
Yarn 1 of 2:
Brand: Rowan
Contents: Wool
Color: Dark brown tweed

Yarn 2 of 2:
Brand: Rowan
Contents: Wool
Color: Light brown tweed

Red-Sleeve Scotland
Pages 74-77
Yarn 1 of 4:
Contents: Wool blend
Color: Red

Yarn 2 of 4:
Contents: Wool blend
Color: Black and white

Yarn 3 of 4:
Contents: Mohair
Color: White

Yarn 4 of 4:
Style: Boucle
Contents: Cotton
Color: White

Long Red Ribbon
Pages 78-81
Yarn 1 of 1:
Brand: Streamers
Style: Ribbon
Contents: Microfiber and poly
Color: Red

Turtlenecks

Random Purl (cream)
Pages 84-87
Yarn 1 of 1:
Brand: Muench
Style: Marokko
Contents: Wool
Color: Beige

Random Purl (purple)
Page 88
Yarn 1 of 1:
Brand: Muench
Style: Marokko
Contents: Wool
Color: Purple

Random Purl (green)
Page 89
Yarn 1 of 1:
Brand: Muench
Style: Marokko
Contents: Wool
Color: Green

Pink and Purple Wide Rib
Pages 90-91
Yarn 1 of 1:
Brand: Colinette
Style: Point 5
Contents: Wool
Color: Pink and purple

Palomino
Pages 92-95
Yarn 1 of 1:
Brand: Colinette
Style: Point 5
Contents: Wool
Color: White and tan

Denim Turtle with Twisted Braid
Pages 96-99
Yarn 1 of 3:
Style: Twisted braid
Color: Denim

Yarn 2 of 3:
Brand: Gedifra Corallo
Style: Ragged edge string
Contents: Cotton and nylon
Color: Green, blue, and beige

Yarn 3 of 3:
Style: Ragged edge ribbon
Contents: Cotton
Color: Gray green

Red Tweed with Contrasting Neck
Pages 100-103
Yarn 1 of 3:
Style: Boucle
Color: Red

Yarn 2 of 3:
Contents: Mohair
Color: Multicolor

Yarn 3 of 3:
Style: Novelty nubby
Color: Multicolor

Aqua Silver
Pages 104-105
Yarn 1 of 2:
Style: Novelty
Color: Multicolor with silver lurex

Yarn 2 of 2:
Contents: Mohair
Color: Aqua

V-Necks

Blue Cable
Pages 108-111
Yarn 1 of 2:
Brand: Organdi
Contents: Linen and synthetic
Color: Light blue

Yarn 2 of 2:
Contents: Cotton
and cashmere
Color: Light blue

Brown and Khaki Cable

Yarn 1 of 3:
Brand: Streamers
Style: Ribbon
Contents: Nylon
Color: Brown

Yarn 2 of 3:
Brand: Streamers
Style: Ribbon
Contents: Nylon
Color: Khaki

Yarn 3 of 3:
Brand: GGH
Style: Ribbon
Contents: Nylon
Color: Tiffany

Rust and Black

Yarn 1 of 1:
Brand: Pettinato
Style: Ribbon shoelace
Contents: Cotton
Color: Rust and
black stripe

Torn Fabric Vest

Yarn 1 of 3:
Brand: Prism
Style: Torn fabric
Color: Multicolor

Yarn 2 of 3:
Style: Eyelash
Color: Multicolor

Yarn 3 of 3
(for crochet trim):
Brand: Anny Blatt
Style: Victoria sheen
ribbon
Color: Black

Fun & Fast Projects

Evening Shawl

Yarn 1 of 2:
Brand: Katia
Style: Chic ribbon
Contents: Merino wool,
nylon, metallic
Color: Hot pink with
gold shimmer

Yarn 2 of 2:
Contents: Mohair
Color: Hot pink

Chunky Scarf

Yarn 1 of 1:
Brand: Muench
Style: Marokko
Contents: Wool
Color: Beige

String Satchel

Yarn 1 of 1:
Style: Twine
Contents: Jute
Color: Beige

Torn Flannel Placemat

Yarn 1 of 1:
Style: Torn flannel
Contents: Cotton
Color: Multicolor

Green Lurex Shell

Yarn 1 of 3:
Brand: Rowan
Style: Lurex
Contents: Viscose
and Lurex
Color: Green

Yarn 2 of 3:
Brand: Rowan
Style: Lurex
Contents: Viscose
and Lurex
Color: Black

Yarn 3 of 3:
Brand: Rowan
Style: Lurex
Contents: Viscose
and Lurex
Color: Off-white

Multi-Chunk Boatneck Shell

Yarn 1 of 1:
Brand: Colinette
Style: Point 5
Contents: Wool
Color: Multicolor

Credits

Red Lips 4 Courage Communications, Inc.
Eileen Cannon Paulin, Catherine Risling,
Rebecca Ittner, Jayne Cosh

Book Editor: Catherine Risling

Stylist: Rebecca Ittner

Book Designer: Deborah Kehoe,
Kehoe + Kehoe Design Associates, Inc., Burlington, VT

Photographer: Denny Nelson

Knitting Consultant: Ellen Liberles

Yarn Shops

Downtown Yarns • New York City, New York
www.downtownyarns.com

The Handworks Gallery • Little Rock, Arkansas
www.handworksgallery.com

Jennifer Knits • Los Angeles, California
www.jenniferknits.com

Kaleidoscope Yarns • Essex Junction, Vermont
www.kaleidoscopeyarns.com

L' Atelier • Santa Monica and Redondo Beach,
California
www.latelier.com

Needlepoint Joint • Ogden, Utah
www.needlepointjoint.com

Needlework Unlimited • Minneapolis, Minnesota
www.needleworkunlimited.com

Personal Threads • Omaha, Nebraska
www.personalthreads.com

Sealed With a Kiss • Guthrie, Oklahoma
www.swakknit.com

Tricoter • Seattle, Washington
www.tricoter.com

Urban Knitworks • Vancouver, B.C.
www.urbanknitworks.com

Wildfiber • Santa Monica, California
www.wildfiber.com

Yarn Barn • Lawrence, Kansas
www.yarnbarn-ks.com

The Yarn Co. • New York City, New York
www.theyarnco.com

About the Authors

A passionate knitter, Kitty Bartholomew also is a famous television decorator. She is loved by millions of viewers who have been watching her on television and attending her personal appearances for more than two decades. Her show, "Kitty Bartholomew: You're Home," launched Home and Garden Television, and the show ran on that network for eight years. Before that, Kitty was a regular on "The Home Show" on ABC, where she built a home from the ground up and tackled many interesting decorating and remodeling projects around the country. She also has appeared on "Oprah." While Kitty is known for her affordable and inventive interior decorating style, she is also celebrated for her wardrobe of more than 70 stylish one-of-a-kind sweaters, handknit by her. Kitty has a background in the fashion industry, and has worked as a clothing designer. Her unique sweaters have been featured on the "Carol Duvall Show" on HGTV, and Kitty has been photographed wearing her sweaters in several magazines, including Woman's Day and Country Home. Kitty can be reached at www.kittybartholomew.com.

Co-author Kathy Price-Robinson is a journalist and book author. She has written about remodeling and decorating for more than 15 years, and her remodeling column for the Los Angeles Times, "Pardon Our Dust," earned a second-place award for best series from the National Association of Real Estate Editors. Plus, "She Said, He Said," a remodeling column she wrote for Homestore.com with her husband, general building contractor Bill Robinson, earned a "Best of the Web" distinction by Forbes.com. Kathy can be reached at www.kathyprice.com.

From Kitty Bartholomew:

I want to thank my late grandmother, Norma King O'Connor, for taking the time to show me how to knit, and for teaching me the basics of this wonderful passion.

Also, I'd like to thank Leslie Stormon and Randy Medall at L' Atelier in Santa Monica and Jennifer Wenger from Jennifer Knits in Los Angeles for their courage to showcase some of the most beautiful and exciting yarns made, yarns that make me want to keep knitting. Thank you Leslie and Randy for allowing us to photograph at your beautiful shop. These knowledgable women showed me that patterns can be custom made quickly and painlessly, which has allowed me the freedom to knit sweaters "my way."

And I want to thank my co-author Kathy Price-Robinson, who is a joy to work with.

From Kathy Price-Robinson:

I want to thank Kitty for her indomitably positive attitude, as well as her endless talent. And I want to thank my husband, Bill Robinson, for listening with great interest to every yarn and knitting story I cared to tell.

Kitty and Kathy want to thank their literary agent, Ted Weinstein, for his intelligence and perseverance. And we'd like to thank the team at Red Lips 4 Courage Communications for their enthusiasm and work on this book: Eileen Cannon Paulin, Rebecca Ittner, and Cathy Risling.

METRIC EQUIVALENCY CHARTS

inches to millimeters and centimeters
mm-millimeters   cm-centimeters

inches	mm	cm	inches	cm	inches	cm
⅛	3	0.3	9	22.9	30	76.2
¼	6	0.6	10	25.4	31	78.7
½	13	1.3	12	30.5	33	83.8
⅝	16	1.6	13	33.0	34	86.4
¾	19	1.9	14	35.6	35	88.9
⅞	22	2.2	15	38.1	36	91.4
1	25	2.5	16	40.6	37	94.0
1¼	32	3.2	17	43.2	38	96.5
1½	38	3.8	18	45.7	39	99.1
1¾	44	4.4	19	48.3	40	101.6
2	51	5.1	20	50.8	41	104.1
2½	64	6.4	21	53.3	42	106.7
3	76	7.6	22	55.9	43	109.2
3½	89	8.9	23	58.4	44	111.8
4	102	10.2	24	61.0	45	114.3
4½	114	11.4	25	63.5	46	116.8
5	127	12.7	26	66.0	47	119.4
6	152	15.2	27	68.6	48	121.9
7	178	17.8	28	71.1	49	124.5
8	203	20.3	29	73.7	50	127.0

yards to meters

yards	meters	yards	meters	yards	meters	yards	meters	yards	meters
⅛	0.11	2⅛	1.94	4⅛	3.77	6⅛	5.60	8⅛	7.43
¼	0.23	2¼	2.06	4¼	3.89	6¼	5.72	8¼	7.54
⅜	0.34	2⅜	2.17	4⅜	4.00	6⅜	5.83	8⅜	7.66
½	0.46	2½	2.29	4½	4.11	6½	5.94	8½	7.77
⅝	0.57	2⅝	2.40	4⅝	4.23	6⅝	6.06	8⅝	7.89
¾	0.69	2¾	2.51	4¾	4.34	6¾	6.17	8¾	8.00
⅞	0.80	2⅞	2.63	4⅞	4.46	6⅞	6.29	8⅞	8.12
1	0.91	3	2.74	5	4.57	7	6.40	9	8.23
1⅛	1.03	3⅛	2.86	5⅛	4.69	7⅛	6.52	9⅛	8.34
1¼	1.14	3¼	2.97	5¼	4.80	7¼	6.63	9¼	8.46
1⅜	1.26	3⅜	3.09	5⅜	4.91	7⅜	6.74	9⅜	8.57
1½	1.37	3½	3.20	5½	5.03	7½	6.86	9½	8.69
1⅝	1.49	3⅝	3.31	5⅝	5.14	7⅝	6.97	9⅝	8.80
1¾	1.60	3¾	3.43	5¾	5.26	7¾	7.09	9¾	8.92
1⅞	1.71	3⅞	3.54	5⅞	5.37	7⅞	7.20	9⅞	9.03
2	1.83	4	3.66	6	5.49	8	7.32	10	9.14

Index